BRANCH
TO
SOUTHMINSTER

Dennis L. Swindale

EARM PUBLICATIONS

a division of East Anglian Railway Museum (Trading) Ltd.

EARM PUBLICATIONS

Chappel & Wakes Colne Station, Colchester, CO6 2DS. Tel. 01206 242524
a division of East Anglian Railway Museum (Trading) Ltd., the trading subsidiary
of East Anglian Railway Museum, a Registered Charity No. 1001579

Publishing History:
First published jointly by the author and the
Stour Valley Railway Preservation Society 1981

Revised and updated edition published by East Anglian Railway Museum 1997

Further revised, updated and expanded edition published by EARM Publications
2008

ISBN 0 95553121 2 0
978 0 9553121 2 0
British Library Cataloguing In Publication Data.
A catalogue record for this book is available from the British Library
© East Anglian Railway Museum 2008
Typeset and designed by EARM Publications

Printed by Crescent Card Company, Tiptree, Colchester, Essex

Acknowledgements

When it was suggested that I write about the Southminster branch line I felt at first that there would be little to record - a rural branch line wending its way through placid countryside, eventually reaching a terminus located 'in the middle of nowhere', lacking the drama of the great main line routes. However, the Southminster branch is one of the few survivors of the old Great Eastern Railway system which is still operating almost in the form envisaged by its builders, and in the course of many interviews I came to appreciate the importance of the line to its users and the affection in which it is held locally. Memories were searched and information freely given, most of which is embodied in the following chapters.

Amongst so many helpful people it seems invidious to single out any, but I must express my grateful thanks to Mr B.D.J. Walsh who allowed me to extract as much information as I required from his article on the railways of the area which appeared in 'The Railway Magazine' over twenty years ago. Mr D. Collins gave up a great deal of his time to write down everything that he knew about the line and Mr. Murray Prior kindly loaned me a unique and irreplaceable document - the diary kept by his grandfather during the building of the line. Mr. 'Chib' Thorp very generously presented me with the tape upon which he had recorded interviews with railway staff at all the stations from Woodham Ferrers to Southminster and useful technical facts came from Leading Railman V. Harrington and Signalman A.W. Hawkes. Retired Guard Freebourn, a grand old gentleman in his eighties, recalled memories of the GER days, and a member of the younger generation of railwaymen, Driver Charlie Dore, provided useful information on present day workings. Mr. Rex Algar, who spent part of his boyhood as the son of a stationmaster on the line, delved into those days for me, and in Burnham and the surrounding area interesting items were supplied by Mrs. P. Bovis, Mr. Bryan R. Symes, Mr. John Randall and local historian Mr. Alf Pyner. Other useful facts were provided by Messrs. Chris Emptage, Harry Paar and Nigel Bowdidge.

Credits for the photographs used appear beneath them and I must thank Dr. Paddy Lacey for allowing me to make free with his collection.

To all those named or unnamed who gave their help, my deepest thanks. Sources consulted were: *The Daily Telegraph, The Essex Chronicle, The Carlisle Journal, Railway Magazine, Essex Countryside, Maldon and Burnham Standard, The Great Eastern Railway Magazine, The Tramways of Southend on Sea* (V.E. Burrows), *Railways of Essex* (A. Smith and T. Williams) and *Locomotives of the GER* (Langley Aldrich).

Dennis L. Swindale April 1981

Acknowledgements for the second edition
Dennis had started revising and updating the book to take into account the electrification and recent years on the branch when he was sadly taken ill and died. This work was taken over by Mick Miller and Rob Boyce, and was nearing completion when Mick died suddenly. It has now been completed, and is published by the East Anglian Railway Museum as a tribute to Dennis, whose encyclopaedic knowledge of the line will be sorely missed and to Mick, for all his efforts on behalf of the Museum. Special thanks must go to the following for their unstinting assistance with this second edition: Dr. Paddy Lacey, Carl Lombardelli, Jeff Morss, John Nash, Ron Quantock, Steve Mew and Mike Miller.

Acknowledgements for the third edition
This edition was revised and updated by Mark House and Rob Boyce, with once again invaluable assistance from Dr. Paddy Lacey without whom the book would never have been revised. Thanks also to Steve Mew, Jeff Morss, John Jolly, J. Ford, Michael Stanbury, Mike Miller and Nathaniel Dodd.

EARM Publications, May 2008

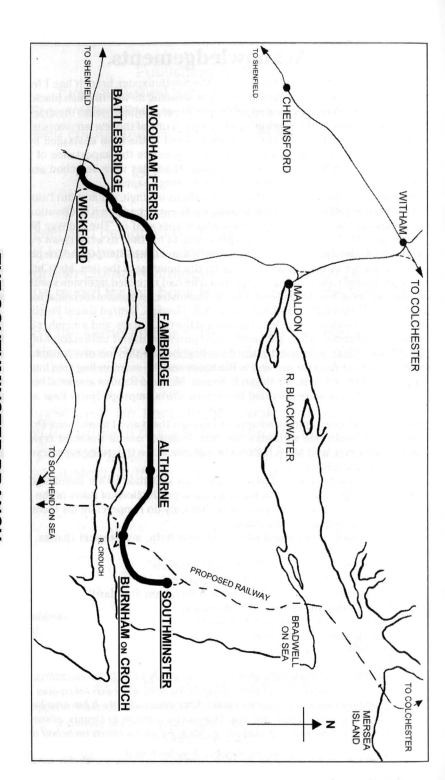

THE SOUTHMINSTER BRANCH

Showing the now closed Branch lines to Maldon

Introduction

The Dengie Peninsula is still one of the loneliest areas in Essex. It is roughly wedge-shaped widening out to the east, where its almost straight coastline faces the North Sea, bordered on its north side by the Blackwater Estuary and by the River Crouch along its southern side. The terrain is mainly level, apart from a ridge along the Crouch valley and some higher ground in the north-east, while major roads are few and winding. Inland is a rich agricultural area of lush fields and tree lined lanes, where the habitations are sparse, whilst, in complete contrast to this, the perimeter of the peninsular consists of lonely marshland, particularly along the seaward side. Here, once away from the major roads, vast arable fields sweep down to the sea wall and only a few isolated farms are to be seen. Beyond the sea wall are the mud flats, where at low water the sea is but a distant line upon the horizon. The flats are the haunt of sea birds and rich in shellfish, but a death trap for the unwary. There are no towns in the Dengie Peninsular, but in the centre of the agricultural area is the large village of Southminster, now a quiet backwater, but in days gone by a busy place of markets and cattle sales. A few miles to the south lies Burnham on Crouch, once a fishing village, but now much larger and a favourite venue for yachtsmen.

Before the coming of the railway to Southminster, communications in the peninsular were slow and wearisome and the roads appalling. In the early 1800s, a Mr. Willsmer ran a horse omnibus every Friday from Southminster to the market at the county town of Chelmsford, a distance of about sixteen miles as the crow flies, but many more along the area's twisting lanes. When the railway line to Maldon opened in 1848, Mr. Willsmer agreed (with financial persuasion) not to run direct to Chelmsford, but to run on Thursdays, Fridays and Saturdays from Burnham to Maldon via Southminster. Even with the rail connection at Maldon, this was still a long and tiring journey over poor roads and gives an indication of the ordeal to which people were subjected if they wished to travel more than a short distance from their place of residence. There were several ferries across both the Crouch and Blackwater, which did cut down journey times for those wishing to travel outside the area, but even to reach them was not easy and the main problem was always the distances to be covered on foot or by horse-drawn transport over muddy, pot-holed roads or tracks. Small wonder that the ordinary person travelled rarely in early Victorian Britain.

Small wonder also that a multitude of railway building proposals flourished as speculators rushed to cash in upon the bonanza created by the prospect of rapid and easy communication. Many of these lines were doomed to failure and to bring financial ruin to their promoters and shareholders, based as they were upon unbridled enthusiasm and lack of technical expertise, and it was not until the amalgamation of these ramshackle early railways into sound and businesslike organisations that they were able to fulfil their early promise of service to both industry and the population.

One of these new and powerful groups was the Great Eastern Railway.

Chapter1: Building the Line

The Great Eastern Railway was almost two railways in one. In North and East London it developed one of the most intensive steam worked passenger services ever known, whilst in the eastern counties it developed fast lines to all the major towns of the area, together with an extensive network of branch lines serving the hitherto remote agricultural regions, a vast storehouse of grain, vegetable and fruit production. Formed in 1862, the GER was by the early 1880's in a position to compete with the London, Tilbury and Southend Railway in the bid to reach Southend, although until 1st July 1880, locomotives of the GER had worked over the LT&SR tracks. In 1883 the GER received Parliamentary powers to build its own line to Southend and to develop the large area of south-east Essex thus far not served by rail.

In fact there had been an earlier proposal to build lines in the same part of the county by the South Essex Railway (SER), which was promoted in the early 1860s. On 8th July 1865 the SER was authorised to build a line, from a junction with the GER at Brentwood, to Southminster, with a branch to Maldon and in the following year additional powers were obtained for a line from Rettendon to the LT&SR at Pitsea. Sufficient capital to undertake construction was never raised however, and the Company was wound up a few years later.

By its Act of 16th July 1883 the Great Eastern Railway was empowered to build a line from Shenfield, via Wickford, to Southend, together with a branch from Wickford to Southminster and a branch from Woodham Ferris to Maldon, there to join the existing Witham to Maldon line at a point to the west of Maldon station. These powers included the construction of triangular junctions at Wickford, Maldon and Witham, permitting through running without reversals between Colchester and Southend. It is thought that there may have been some military considerations underlying the planning of this through route.

The line from Shenfield to Wickford opened to goods traffic on 19th November 1888 and to passenger traffic from 1st January 1889 – a bright and frosty day, but the departure of the first passenger train seemed to arouse little excitement, the only passengers being two ladies and a policeman. Powers had been obtained in the GER Act of 8th August 1887 for an extension until 16th July 1890 for time to complete the remaining lines, known as the 'New Essex Lines', and work went on apace on all three routes to meet this date. In fact, the Southminster line was finished first, opening for goods services on 1st June 1889, whilst both the Southend and Maldon lines opened on 1st October 1889. The track was double from Shenfield to Wickford, there dividing into two single lines to Southminster and Southend.

From the junction at Wickford (28 1/2 miles from London and 11 3/4 miles from Southend), the Southminster branch extended north-eastwards and then almost due east to Althorne, the line running parallel with and close to the River Crouch until it swung into a curve through Burnham, taking up a northerly direction on the last stretch to Southminster, 16 1/2 miles from Wickford. No powers were ever granted to extend the line through to Bradwell on Sea on the Blackwater

Estuary, which is surprising considering the Great Eastern Railway's extensive maritime interests.

Despite the sparse population along the line, the Southminster branch was well equipped with stations – at Battlesbridge (2$1/2$ miles), Woodham Ferris (5 miles), Fambridge (8 miles), Althorne (11 miles), Burnham on Crouch (14 miles) and Southminster (16$1/2$ miles). The stations were of a standard pattern and all of brick construction, each being equipped with a goods yard and passing loop. There was also a signal box at each station and a goods shed at Battlesbridge, Burnham and Southminster. In addition, there were goods sidings at Hogwell (between Woodham Ferris and Fambridge) and at Creeksea (to the west of Burnham).

The contractors, Walter Scott and Co., had obtained from the Great Eastern Railway Company a contract to build forty miles of railway line and a part of this mileage was the Southminster branch. In charge of the Burnham section of the line and, after its completion, of the whole branch was a Thomas Middleton, who had been connected with Walter Scott and Co., for a period of twenty three years and who was a man of vast experience in the building of both docks and railways, and although most of his work was carried out in the northern part of the British Isles, he was also in charge of the construction of the Stour Valley Line. (His career is outlined in Appendix 1).

One of Thomas Middleton's employees kept a log and recorded some aspects of the building of the Southminster branch, and happily this unique

Woodham Ferris station in its heyday. Beyond the signals the Maldon Branch lies straight ahead and the Southminster line branches off to the right. (Paddy Lacey collection)

document survives to the present day. From it we were able to obtain a vivid picture of the work involved and indeed the speed at which it was carried out. Although the log applies only to the Burnham section, it is indicative of what occurred along the whole line and it is easy to envisage the furious activity which descended upon an area which had seen little change of tempo in the preceding centuries. Gangs of hard swearing, hard fighting and hard drinking navvies descended upon unworldly hamlets, carts and wagons of materials turned country lanes into quagmires, cuttings were hacked through rising ground and embankments thrust out over marshes. With the scarcity of houses in the area, hutted camps sprang up at various points along the workings, although huts is a rather grand description for the squalid erections in which these colourful characters slept and drank themselves into oblivion on pay nights. But, at their work they were superb and nothing withstood their determined efforts to push on over any terrain.

In one respect the builders of the line were very lucky – it ran close to the River Crouch on the banks of which were hards upon which materials could be unloaded from boats. In the late 1800s, where no railways existed, most bulk materials were carried by water and the seas around East Anglia and the Thames Estuary were the domain of the Thames Barge. These graceful craft sailed into every port, river and creek of the south-eastern coastline, their brown sails standing starkly above the green grassland of the marshes as they threaded their way along some invisible river or creek. Manned by only a small crew, sometimes just the

Battlesbridge station was sometimes known as Rettendon station. A view in GER days in the eastwards direction with the goods shed in the distance. (EARM collection)

master and a boy the barges were able by virtue of their flat bottoms to take the ground safely, which was ideal for unloading purposes as they could edge in almost to the sea wall at high water and sit upright on the hard as the tide receded, permitting carts and wagons to come alongside for off-loading the cargo.

Across the Thames Estuary, in north Kent, were situated large brick fields where the barges maintained a shuttle service to bring in cargoes of Stock bricks, Blue bricks and copings.

For the Burnham section of the line, the hard at Stokes Hall, to the west of Burnham, was used and the barges started to offload on 2nd November 1886 continuing until 31st July 1888. It was ironic that the barges were hastening the demise of their own water-borne trade in being used to carry materials for building the line, for before the advent of the railways, they carried amongst other goods, agricultural produce including hay, into London for the capital's thousands of work horses, bringing back various cargoes including the end-product of the hay, horse manure, for fertilizing the fields.

The bricks came in first – almost a million and a half of them for the Burnham section alone, to be followed by second hand sleepers, track laying tools and other gear for building a temporary track. Then followed the permanent gear and arriving at Stokes Hall were cargoes of permanent sleepers from Lowestoft, chairs, rails and spikes from the north, and in amongst the barges came some laden ketches, a schooner and a couple of early steamships. These larger craft unloaded part of their cargoes into smaller boats, being able then to come in closer to the shore. In passing it is interesting to note that a Captain Dennis arrived at Stokes Hall in the barge *Bonetta* with a load of bricks from Halstow, in north Kent, and then arrived with another load of bricks, this

A pre-1914 view of the neat station buildings at Battlesbridge, seen from the approach drive. (D. Penn collection)

time from London, in the barge *Alice Mary* on the following day. It is possible that there were two captains of the same name, but if not, Captain Dennis moved very swiftly indeed! However, two other barges had arrived with bricks from Halstow on the preceding day and two days before, so perhaps the redoubtable captain sailed back immediately to Halstow on one of them, took a train to London from north Kent and sailed the *Alice Mary* to Burnham on the following day. If that is what happened, it serves to indicate at what speed the construction of the line was pressed forward.

With the cessation of the barge traffic to the line, materials began to be distributed to stations along its length, and from the log it would appear that the permanent track was by then in position, most of the transferred materials being intended for the construction of pointwork and sidings in the various station yards. On 4th October 1888 Burnham received its first works train, which left timbers and sleepers at various places, including Althorne yard, No. 10 cutting, Creeksea siding and Burnham and Fambridge yards. A second works train ran on the same day carrying rails for Burnham yard and shortly thereafter materials came in from Maldon for the pointwork in Southminster yard. From the notes, therefore, it would be a fair guess that the 'Burnham section' comprised the stretch of line from Althorne station to Southminster station including Burnham station and Creeksea siding. As an example of the costings of the period, the total expenditure for the erection at Southminster of coal bunkers, cattle pens, a water reservoir and some cottages, amounted to £13,500.

With the stations and bridges built, the trackwork completed and the signalling installed the line was now ready for inspection prior to opening for the carriage firstly of goods and then of passengers.

Chapter 2: The Route Described

Wickford Station, much altered since it was built, but still of the same basic platform layout, is situated upon a short stretch of level track which, at the time of opening of the Southminster branch, was double as far as this point before diverging into single lines to Southend and Southminster. (Doubling commenced on the Southend line in 1901). Originally there were substantial brick buildings with canopies running their entire length, upon both platforms and at the London end a latticed covered footbridge joined the platforms, which had bays at the outer faces. The station nameboard read 'Wickford Junction, Change here for Burnham, Southminster and Maldon'. The goods yard was at the London end of the station, on the down side, and had outlet to the down main line at the country end together with a connection to the up main line at the London end. Opposite the yard, on the up side, was the loco yard and a 50ft turntable.

Trains coming off the Southminster branch entered the up side bay and were shunted into the down bay after the departure of the connecting trains. R.J. Ford remembers as a child being occasionally allowed (unofficially!) to be in charge of this move and writes "The ultimate excitement for a ten or eleven year old was at Wickford in the transfer of the three coaches from the Up bay to the Down bay with

Y14 647 with the 3.5pm ECS ex Southminster near Wickford, 22nd April 1911 (Ken Nunn collection, courtesy of the Loconotive Club of Great Britain)

the procedure as follows: on arrival in the Up bay the engine was uncoupled, then the three coaches were propelled up the hill across the Up line onto the Down line as far as necessary to clear the points into the Down bay. At this point the brakes were applied to the coaches and the engine proceeded up the Down line into the siding on the London side of the station where it remained until the London train arrived. Passengers alighted for the Southminster line and the train proceeded towards Southend. Now came the exciting part – with this eleven year old in charge of the brake as the three coaches under gravity ran down the incline into the bay. The instructions from Guard Wright are still in my mind!". A feature of the country end of the station was a group of three gantries each carrying two signals which controlled movements where the bays joined the main line.

The station buildings have been altered several times over the years. At the time of the electrification of the Southend line, the down side buildings were rearranged and the entrance hall enlarged, and in 1978 the up side buildings were replaced by a new structure and the bay platform lengthened. The old signals were replaced by colour lights in the late 1960s and overhead wires and their supports are very evident.

The once small village of Wickford is now immensely increased in size, large housing estates having sprung up in the 1920s and 1930s and since the end of the Second World War, the whole area now resembling an outer London suburb which has been transported bodily into the Essex countryside and many people commute from here to Southend as well as to London.

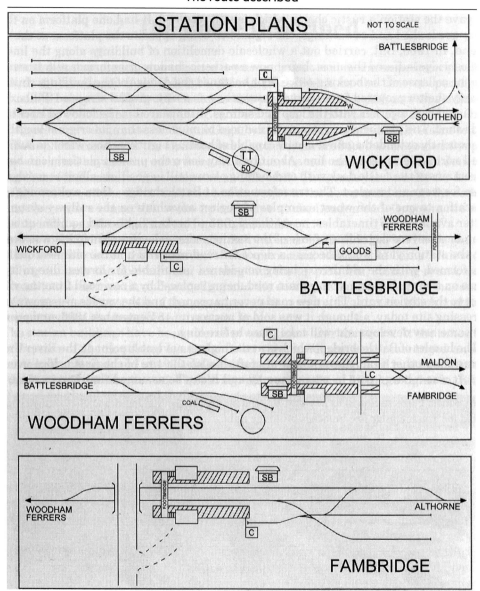

STATION PLANS — NOT TO SCALE

WICKFORD

BATTLESBRIDGE

WOODHAM FERRERS

FAMBRIDGE

About half a mile beyond Wickford station, the Southminster branch leaves the main line in a north easterly direction, this curve being the remaining part of the triangular junction, the upper sides of which joined at Belchamps Junction. The Fanton curve of the junction was lifted after the through Colchester to Southend service ceased in 1894, but a siding was later laid approximately upon the formation of this curve and served the factories on the Wick Lane industrial estate. Also in

STATION PLANS

NOT TO SCALE

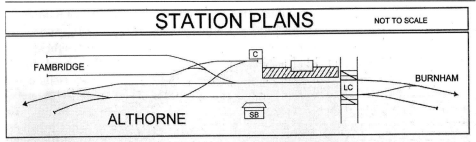

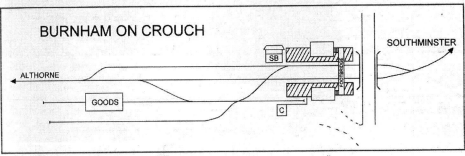

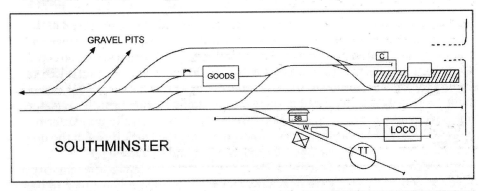

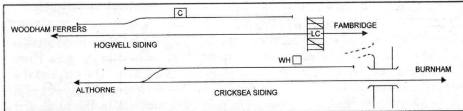

this area, between Wickford and Shotgate, one bridge under the line was so low that when open-topped double deck buses ran through conductors would give those travelling upon the upper deck instructions to duck their heads as the bus approached the arch! Needless to say, this hazard has long since gone and passengers on the top deck of present day buses are in no danger of decapitation.

Shaking off the last of the built-up outskirts of Wickford, the line passes through open fields, climbing at 1 in 100 for three quarters of a mile, after which there is a similarly graded descent leading to a level stretch which brings the line to Battlesbridge station.

Battlesbridge station, 2½ miles from Wickford, was considered by many to be the most attractive of the branch. A curving drive led up to the station forecourt from the Rettendon to Battlesbridge road which passed under the line at the Wickford end of the single platform. The station buildings were similar to others on the line but the seclusion of the site gave the station a rustic charm which is still retained. It had one platform on the up side, goods shed and two sidings, the signal box being opposite the platform at the country end. In 1968, BR carried out a wholesale demolition of buildings along the line and Battlesbridge suffered the most, being now a pathetic shadow of its former self. It was said that the collapse of the booking office floor hastened the demise of the buildings. Initially the only shelter provided for waiting passengers was a tiny, graffiti scrawled 'pillbox' hut. The signal box, together with the loop and sidings, disappeared – to be followed later by the goods shed. The platform was originally reduced to much less than its original length, but subsequently extended again. It is now capable of holding eight coaches, which is sufficient for all normal services on the line. About half way down the present platform can be seen the remains of the cattle dock with end loading plates still in position, albeit somewhat the worse for wear and neglect. The transformation at Battlesbridge – from a charming country station to one of the worst examples of neglect anywhere on the railway system: no shelter available, no timetables, no station signs and broken lights and equipment boxes – is the most severe degrading of any of the stations along the line. In 1979 it was decided that the station yard would become a depot for road material and the site was due to be transformed, with the old drive – being considered unsuitable for lorries, due to its entrance on a sharp bend on a busy main road – being replaced by a new road from the village direct to the station yard. This new road never happened, and the yard is overgrown and a depressing site today, although it was sold at auction on 18 September 1996. However, no new development has yet taken place.

The hamlet of Battlesbridge, which is at the highest navigable point on the River Crouch for anything other than the smallest of craft, is also the site of the first bridge over the river. It was a barge port in years gone by and it can be assumed that barges came into Battlesbridge in connection with the building of the line. There are two mills and two inns in the village and, at the present time, several antique shops, but the post office closed in the 1960s. The railway bridge over the road is something of a menace in these days of juggernaut lorries and is frequently hit by high vehicles, on one occasion being moved out of alignment. As with the bridge between Wickford and Shotgate, bus conductors used to advise passengers on double deck buses to duck when approaching it! The roadway is also liable to flooding, at which times a lengthy detour through Wickford is necessary, but this problem was solved by the opening of a new by-pass in 1981.

Leaving Battlesbridge station the line continues with only negligible gradients and through pleasant but unspectacular countryside until Woodham Ferrers (until 1st October 1913, Woodham Ferris), station is entered, five miles from Wickford. Despite its name, the station is in fact situated in South Woodham Ferrers, Woodham Ferrers being upon a hill almost a mile away. The station adjoins the main street of the original village, this road leading to the River Crouch and, in years gone by, a ferry to Hullbridge on the far bank. Before the coming of the railway South Woodham Ferrers consisted of only a few scattered dwellings, but in the 1920s and 1930s there was much indiscriminate building and the village became widely scattered, staying thus until the commencement of a New Town in 1975, which has completely transformed the area.

Woodham Ferrers station was the junction of the Southminster and Maldon lines, the latter leading off straight ahead beyond the level crossing at the eastern end of the station, whilst the Southminster branch curved away towards the Crouch valley. It was a substantial station with two platforms connected by a footbridge and with a signal box on the Wickford end of the up platform. There was a goods yard on the down side and a loco yard, with turntable, on the up side. By 1911 the turntable was disused as tank engines were used on the Maldon trains: its date of removal is unknown, but it is not listed in the 1923 Grouping station facilities register. During the reduction of the station buildings along the line, those upon the up platform, together with the signal box and footbridge, were removed as was the track through the up platform and in the yard. There is now no trace of the loco yard and turntable pit.

Althorne station in June 1960 (Douglas Thompson, EARM collection)

The building remaining at Woodham Ferrers is the station house, the majority of which is boarded up and in a poor state of repair. However, part of it continues to be used on weekday mornings as a ticket office. All other buildings have been removed, but there is still a GER canopy, supported by ornate Great Eastern posts. A waiting shelter is situated some two-thirds of the way along the platform: nominally of glass and metal, all glass has been long broken and it is open to the elements. The creation of the New Town might have turned events here almost full circle, as rumours existed that the up platform might be reinstated: however, this has come to nothing, although traces of the old up platform are discernible through the undergrowth. In mid-1980 an item in the local newspaper reported that BR were considering the building of a new halt in the industrial area to the east of the town, although this too has never come to fruition. The level crossing gates and starter signals formerly provided here were operated from a two-lever frame close to the gates and on the up side, the person operating them being provided with the luxury of a brick-built crossing keeper's hut. Initially the level crossing at the station was converted to 'automatic open' status from 9 March 1986 – a change which generated much local opposition from local residents who viewed it as a potential safety hazard: the subject was even raised in Parliament. The crossing keeper's hut was demolished at about this time. Partly, but not wholly, as a result of the concerns over the crossing, it was eventually converted to 'automatic half barrier' status with effect from 4th April 1993. A Portakabin type hut is provided for the necessary technical equipment.

Fambridge station in June 1960 (Douglas Thompson, EARM collection)

On both the eastern and western sides of the New Town orbital roads cross the line over new bridges immediately adjacent to Salter's Crossing and Fenn Crossing respectively, and the gates at these crossings have been replaced with simple lifting barriers.

After a short curve out of Woodham Ferrers station the line now heads eastwards in a straight stretch of six miles along the edge of the riverside marshland, rising after 1½ miles, at 1 in 130/100 for three quarters of a mile before dropping towards Fambridge station at 1 in 110/130. There is a change of scenery along this stretch as, after leaving the agricultural environs of Woodham Ferrers, the line enters an area of sweeping vistas. On the north side can be seen the Burnham road running along a ridge of higher ground whilst to the south the view is bounded by the low hills well beyond the far bank of the River Crouch. The saltings extend to the actual railway embankment, a mass of glittering mud and dull green plant life at low water, a sail-dotted expanse of glittering wavelets when the tide is high.

On the north side of the line a glimpse of the old cattle dock which served Hogwell Siding can be seen, lingering on in the grass. The siding was built for agricultural use, but was closed before 1939. Access to the siding was via a ground frame controlled by an Annett's key carried by the train crew. There is

Fambridge in July 2005, with 321332 forming an Up service. The present day buildings can be seen on both platforms (EARM collection)

still a level crossing hereto leading to the headwaters of Stow Creek and its crumbling jetty which is complete with the forlorn remains of an old sailing barge, the 'CERF'. Apart from constructing the crossing, the GER were obliged to build two farm cottages at this point as part of the landowner's price for the crossing of his property. Although the cottages therefore resemble railway employee's accommodation, they are in fact, not so.

A slightly raised, tree-girt peninsula appears ahead and at its tip sprouts a forest of masts from the boatyards river moorings and the marina at North Fambridge, a village with a long main street leading to a riverside inn and, until the late 1950s, a ferry to South Fambridge. The station is situated at the north end of the village and is now the passing place for trains in peak periods. Its two platforms are in a cutting which shallows to the east and at the other end there is a road bridge over the double track.

There were buildings on both platforms, with a connecting footbridge close to the road bridge, and a signal box just beyond the end of the down platform and a goods yard. The station many times won prizes for the beauty of its gardens and on a soft summer's day it was a pleasure to wait for the white plume of smoke across the green marshland whilst drinking in the riotous colours and the heady scents of the massed flowers. Now the station is but a shadow of its former self, with even the signal box swept away as part of the modernisation. The buildings, with their ornate and shady canopies, have been swept away and initially only two small buildings remained, and on the down side there was no protection at all for the luckless passenger caught in a downpour.

However, towards the end of 1985 a new shelter was provided on the down platform, at a cost of £1125, the cost being met jointly by Maldon District Council

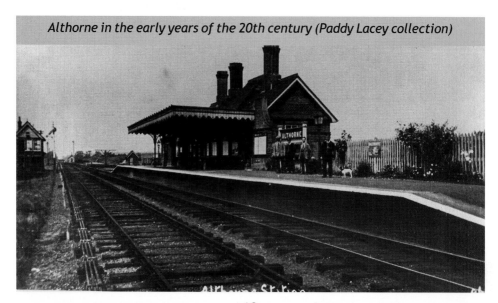

Althorne in the early years of the 20th century (Paddy Lacey collection)

and the British Railway's Board Central Environment Fund. Recent new housing development near the station has helped add to the line's traffic.

With its polished brass and gleaming paint, the splendid GER signalbox was a pleasure to visit. The frame contained eight working and two spare levers, and the box marked the junction of the two single line sections into which the branch is divided, the Fambridge to Wickford section being worked with Tyer's Key equipment and the Fambridge to Southminster section by Railway Signal Company's Brass Staff. Each end of the Fambridge loop was protected by a Distant, Home and Starter signal, the Distants being in the fixed 'on' position as were all Distant signals on the line. The passing loop remains, but it is – as with all signalling on the line – controlled from the signalling centre at Liverpool Street. The signalbox was taken out of use in December 1985 and demolished in February 1986.

For half a mile beyond Fambridge station there is a descending gradient of 1 in 110/300, followed by a short level stretch, a sharp rise of 1 in 100 for three-quarters of a mile and a gentle descent into Althorne station.

The stretch of line from Fambridge to Althorne runs as straight as an arrow and once again the passenger is treated to a panoramic view of wide marshland. In summer the sense of space is almost overwhelming – a great sweep of blue sky, flecked with puffs of white cloud, is reflected in equally blue and sparkling water dotted with sails of various colours, whilst in winter, when the sky is a riot of sunset's orange and gold, a purple grey mist will come creeping up from the river and the marshland features will melt and dissolve. Seen from the road above, the train cutting across this dreamlike landscape resembles a chain of lighted lanterns. On the sharp rise before Althorne, bushes grow close to the line and in the dusk rabbits gambol and frolic on the track until the train is almost upon them.

Althorne station is another ghost bereft of all but the last fragments of its buildings. It has been called the 'station on the marsh' and undoubtedly is the loneliest station on the line, situated at the end of a narrow pot-holed lane which leads steeply down from the Burnham road. The village is at least half a mile away. In its heyday, Althorne station was all that a country station should be; the waiting room floor gleamed and gave off pleasant odours of polish there were fresh flowers from the tiny garden on the table, and on the waiting room walls hung framed certificates for 'The Best Kept Station'. There was a passing loop, a goods yard on the down side and an attractive GER signal box on the up side. These have now all gone: initially, only a small shelter (previously the lamp room) and the toilet block remained, although these too have now gone and been replaced by a brick built waiting shelter, which has the BR 'double arrow' insignia in brick. Initially capable of holding five coaches, the platform was extended in Spring 1987 to hold eight coaches. In the old yard, dark traces of the lifted sidings are still just about recognisable. The road to the station continues over the line by means of an automatic crossing: prior to this being installed, a gated crossing was in place which had to be opened and closed by those taking vehicles across, but which was locked for trains from a two lever frame at the end of the platform: the other lever controlling the station signals. The road then becomes a rough track leading to a few waterside dwellings and to Bridgemarsh Creek. There are a few railway cottages near to the station, but these are now privately owned. In late 1996, the former station house was renovated.

The short road to the creek was sometimes used for the transport of heavy equipment by rail and water in the days when roads on both sides of the River Crouch were either rudimentary or non-existent. When some very heavy steam-driven agricultural machinery was needed on one of the islands lying beyond the Rivers Crouch and Roach, it was offloaded from the train at Althorne, manhandled along the road to the creek upon greased timbers and then loaded onto a barge to complete the journey to its destination. There is also a story, believed to be authentic, that a derailed locomotive was removed from the vicinity of the station by the same method. This was in the days when tasks which would now be carried out by sophisticated plant were achieved by the usage of the simplest equipment and a prodigious amount of human muscle.

Leaving Althorne station, the line curves into a straight section which heads south-east and rises continuously at 1 in 200/100 for nearly two miles, still following the curve of the River Crouch and in a cutting for most of that distance. The lane to Stokes Hall hard is passed early on in the cutting and then, as the line begins to curve through 180 degrees towards Burnham, the site of Creeksea (originally Cricksea

N7 69616 at Burnham on Crouch, Southminster-bound (Paddy Lacey collection)

Ferry) Siding is passed. This was a similar siding to Hogwell Siding, built for agricultural use, but in this case was provided with a weighbridge and office. When the siding was used, a porter was sent from Burnham with the token, returning thence after operations on the siding had ceased. There is little to see of the site now, although the course of the siding is still plain. The weigh office remained in isolation for some time after the siding was lifted but now that too has disappeared.

The line now runs further away from the river and enters Burnham on Crouch in a north-easterly direction, there being only gentle undulations in the gradient for the rest of the distance to the terminus. The station at Burnham on Crouch is quite large and the track was double through its two platforms. The buildings were of a similar type to those of the other stations on the line and there was a goods yard, with shed, on the up side, whilst the signal box was opposite the yard entry on the down side. The platforms were connected with the usual latticed and covered footbridge at the country end, close to the bridge which carries the road into Burnham over the line. Adjacent to the yard are the remains of the Mildmay Ironworks which contributed a large amount of goods traffic but which, as far as it can be ascertained, did not have its own siding.

The only buildings now remaining are on the up side, those opposite succumbing to the demolition men as they worked their way along the line. The

Burnham on Crouch station in July 2005 (EARM collection)

down track was also lifted and all that can be seen is the weed-grown down platform. Looking at this it is difficult to visualise the beautiful gardens of days past, which were so attractive that no less than twenty awards were won between the early 1920s and the mid 1960s. The remaining buildings received some attention during 1996, with the windows being boarded up, although a ticket office remains open on Monday to Friday mornings. New station signs have recently been installed.

Burnham on Crouch itself has grown from a remote fishing village into one of the premier yachting centres of the East Coast and the location of several famous yacht clubs. Its lengthy High Street contains many attractive old buildings and there are further buildings of interest, including three waterfront inns and several boat-building sheds, along the riverside promenade. From an 1881 population of 2130 it grew to 4000 persons in 1952, although there has since been some considerable housing developments on the outskirts: by 1981 the population had increased to 6308. However, by 2001 it had fallen slightly to 5900, and as Burnham has no through road it would seem unlikely that it will experience any further substantial increase.

The line now heads north/north-east towards the terminus, passing through pleasant but undistinguished agricultural land, the gradients being negligible until the last gentle slope down into Southminster station. This was a pleasurable place at which to end the journey along the line as the station remained reasonably

Southminster view towards station signal box with station beyond c1905. The water column & tower are on the right hand side, engine shed to left behind signal box. (Photograph courtesy of Historical Model Railway Society)

unaltered in the first phase of 'rationalisation', and was spared such drastic demolition as affected some stations. Some of the original buildings are still intact, although boarded up and some windows have received the attention of local vandals. The platform canopy remains. On the down side the goods yard and shed were initially retained, although the goods shed has now gone. The ticket office remained; open on Monday to Friday mornings only: this was closed in 1992 as an economy measure. There is, however, a staff mess room at the station to which train crews have access when their train 'lays over' there. The loco sidings, shed and turntable have disappeared from the up side. The signal box – a typical GER example – stood a little way from the station, and remained in reasonable condition until the end of its days. A comparatively recent addition here was a large gantry for loading flasks of nuclear waste brought by road from Bradwell Nuclear Power Station, before transferring to rail for the journey to Sellafield. Sidings were also installed here leading to nearby gravel pits, although this traffic ceased in 1979 and the sidings were subsequently lifted.

Being on the down side only, the station buildings and platforms resemble a through station but, as stated earlier, there is no record of the GER ever applying to take the line further and across the end of the track the Company installed a length of their 'unclimbable' iron fencing.

Southminster in July 2005 (EARM collection)

Southminster is still a fairly sleepy place. The population in 1952 was only 1403 persons, although some housing development has since taken place and the 1981 population was 3206: further increases saw it reach 3709 by 2001. Recent developments have included new housing adjacent to the station. The main street leads down to the station and then onto the marshes. Near to the station are the 'Railway Hotel' and the 'Station Arms', and a small industrial estate stands across the road from the end of the track. It does not seem likely that Southminster will ever greatly increase its size and the pre-war cry of the station staff to passengers, as the branch line train coasted into the platform with a last tired hiss of steam, would not come amiss today – "Southminster, End of the World!".

Chapter 3: Life On The Line: The Opening and The Early Days

Contemporary press reports in 1889 of the opening of the line were very positive, and are given below:

"THE DENGIE HUNDRED RAILWAY: OPENED FOR GOODS TRAFFIC

The first train passed along the line on Thursday, the 30th May. It contained the station masters, porters, and signalmen, who are to do duty at the new stations. The names of the station masters are as follows: Southminster Mr C Leather, late a relieving station master, Ipswich; Burnham, Mr F B Thain, late chief clerk in the goods department at Lowestoft; Althorne, Mr Sidney William Pryke (brother of Police Inspector Pryke of Rochford); late chief clerk in the goods department at Stoke Newington; Fambridge Mr H Pallant, late of Bury St Edmunds; Woodham, Mr F W Avery, late of Worsted; and Battles Bridge, Mr F R Lilley, late chief booking clerk at Chelmsford. The train left Wickford at midday, and the passengers were safely deposited at the various stations. The arrangements were ably supervised by Mr J Flower, the courteous District Superintendent from Ipswich, with whom were Mr J Hunt, telegraph inspector of Ipswich, Mr Hyde, signal inspector of London, and Inspector Norman of Ipswich.

The first goods train: the scene at Southminster

On Friday afternoon several of the tradesmen of Southminster were busy carting empties down to the station ready for the first goods train, which was timed to arrive at Southminster at 3.20 on Saturday afternoon and to leave again at 4pm. A large number of the inhabitants were on the platform to witness the arrival of the train, and, after waiting a considerable time, steam was discerned in the distance, and amid a scene of great excitement there came puffing into the station one of the contractors' engines with two ballast wagons. The disappointment was so great that most of the onlookers marched off in disgust, and someone suggested that it ought to have been 1st April instead of 1st of June. A number, however, stayed on, determined to see the finish, and were rewarded for their pains by seeing a very respectable locomotive arrive with cattle trucks and everything complete at 4.30. No time was lost in disposing of the cargo, and in making arrangements to load again ready for departure. The first to get everything on board was Mr James Gale of Bradwell on Sea, who sent a consignment of 70 very fine Oxford down shearlings. It was very pleasing to see Mr Gale quite himself again after his recent severe accident. Mr Charles Croxon, of Reddings, also sent 30 shearlings, making 100 in all. There was also a consignment of wool for Wales. After pulling up at the goods station to take in the parcels and empties sent by Messrs J S Prior, W Harvey and Son, Samuel Pipe and Son, and others, the first goods train steamed out of Southminster at 5.25. There would have been a great many more sheep sent, but some of the farmers were under the impression that there would have been a Sunday service of trains. This is not the intention of the company however. The service, at any rate for a month, will consist of one luggage train per day, leaving about 4.30pm, to be run by one of the contractor's engines as far as Wickford. According to the latest reliable reports the passenger service will exceed expectations. It is said that as many as six trains will run each way per day.

The scene at Burnham

A large number of people assembled to witness the arrival of the first train. There was a goodly display of bunting, and on the train reaching the station loud cheering was indulged in. The freight consisted of fruit empties, consigned to Messrs W Newman, J Camping & Co., and of goods for Messrs W Cater, A Newman and other tradesmen. There were also a number of cattle trucks. The station here is replete with every accommodation. There is also a goods shed, 42 yards by 15 yards, and four cottages for porters and signal men. The signals will be conducted on McKenzie and Holland's patent principles. The cattle pens are spacious and well suited to the requirements, and the general arrangements are well nigh completed. Gas has been laid on to the station. Mr H J Cooke, of the Star Hotel, has been appointed agent for the collection and delivery of goods. During the present month there will be one train only for goods. It will leave Wickford at 1.25 and arrive at Burnham at 3.0, returning to Burnham from Southminster at 4.10 and leaving at 4.20."

The official opening for passengers was greeted with due ceremony:

"THE DENGIE HUNDRED RAILWAY: OPENING FOR PASSENGER TRAFFIC

On Monday the Great Eastern Railway extension from Wickford to Southminster was opened for passenger traffic. The new line is a few chains over 16 miles in length, and has stations at Battles Bridge, Woodham Ferris, North Fambridge,

Althorne, Burnham and Southminster. Together with the Southend and Maldon branches, which are not yet completed, the construction has cost nearly half a million pounds. The contractors were Messrs Walter Scott and Co of Newcastle on Tyne, and the satisfactory way in which they have carried out their work is proved by the first class certificate given by Major-General Hutchinson of the Board of Trade as the result of an official inspection, which took place on Thursday and Friday. The opening for passenger traffic on Monday was a matter of deep interest to the people of the district, and the trains arrived and departed amid great excitement. The towns of Burnham and Southminster were decorated with bunting and evergreens, and part of the day was devoted to holiday making, the shops at these places closing at one o'clock. At Southminster a complimentary banquet was given to the leading officials of the railway, together with the contractors and others, and there was also a flower show, and, in the evening, a grand display of fireworks. The trains, particularly in the afternoon, were crowded, many inhabitants of the district taking their first railway journey. In order to make the day a memorable one in the lives of the children of Burnham, Messrs A B and W A Croxon kindly treated those between the ages of five and twelve years to a trip to Wickford and back, and Mr J S Prior did the same for the little ones of Southminster. The train conveying them consisted of seventeen carriages and was drawn by two engines. The children numbered over 700, nearly 500 belonging to Burnham. The scene at Burnham was very busy, there not being sufficient accommodation in the long train for all the children. They had to be crowded into the carriages, some had to ride in the brake van, and one or two of those in charge of the party rode on the engine. The Burnham Temperance Brass Band, under Mr G Trussell, accompanied the excursion. One old lady, named Courtman, 91 years of age, who had never before seen a railway train, was carried onto the bridge near the station, from which point she saw the start.

The first passenger train to pass over the line (goods trains have been running since 1st June) was timed to leave Southminster at 8.15 and to reach Wickford at 9.4. A crowd of people assembled to see the departure, and about fifty persons anxious to have the distinction of riding in the first train took tickets. Not more than twenty went from Burnham. The journey was completed without the slightest mishap, and the train reached Wickford with a punctuality which could well be followed on every other line."

An interesting Sunday working from 1891 comprised trains from Blackwall at 8.52 a.m. and from Fenchurch Street at 9.07 a.m. These trains combined at Shenfield, but split again at Wickford into Southminster and Southend portions, returning as two individual trains in the evening, leaving Southminster at 6.20 p.m. for Fenchurch Street and Southend at 6.35 p.m. for Blackwall. On Sundays in 1892 there was a fast train between Fenchurch Street and Southminster, calling only at Burnham on Crouch between Wickford and Southminster.

In early 1891 tragedy struck at Wickford, where Thomas Middleton received fatal injuries in the classic type of accident which has been responsible for the

Wickford	8.30		10.8		1.9		5.26		8.31	
Battlesbridge	8.38		10.15		1.16		5.33		8.38	
Woodham Ferris arr	8.44		10.21		1.22		5.39		8.44	
Woodham Ferris dep	8.45	9.3	10.22	10.25	1.23	1.26	5.40	5.43	8.45	8.48
Cold Norton		9.12		10.34		1.35		5.52		8.57
Maldon West		9.22		10.46		1.45		6.2		9.7
Maldon East		9.25		10.49		1.48		6.5		9.10
Fambridge	9.10		10.30		1.31		5.48		8.53	
Althorne	9.20		10.38		1.39		5.56		9.1	
Burnham	9.34		10.47		1.48		6.5		9.10	
Southminster	9.40		10.52		1.53		6.10		9.15	

								SO*		
Southminster		8.20		11.29			3.2			6.45
Burnham		8.27		11.36			3.9			6.52
Althorne		8.36		11.45			3.18			7.1
Fambridge		8.45		11.54			3.27			7.10
Maldon East	8.25		9.45	11.34		3.7			6.50	
Maldon West	8.30		9.50	11.39		3.12		4.59	6.55	
Cold Norton	8.40		10.0	11.49		3.22		5.9	7.5	
Woodham Ferris arr	8.50	8.53	10.10	11.59	12.2	3.32	3.35	5.19	7.15	7.18
Woodham Ferris dep		8.54			12.3		3.36	5.20		7.19
Battlesbridge		9.2			12.11		3.44	5.28		7.27
Wickford		9.9			12.18		3.51			7.34

SO* - Saturdays only, Colchester to Southend-on-Sea

On Saturdays a train will leave Battlesbridge at 11.5am for Maldon (West) calling at Woodham Ferris and Cold Norton, in connection with the Southend to Colchester Market train.

The first passenger timetable, commencing 1st July 1889

deaths of so many railwaymen over the years. He stepped clear of an incoming goods train only to be knocked down by an empty carriages train on the adjoining line, several of the vehicles passing over his right leg, damaging it so much that amputation above the knee was required. The shock of the accident was too much for a person of Mr. Middleton's advanced years and he died soon after at his Burnham home. It seems a great shame that one who had been so concerned with the building of the line should not survive longer to see it in operation.

The through route from Southend to Colchester, via the two Maldon branches and the Southminster branch between Wickford and Woodham Ferris, lasted only until 1894 and operated only on Saturdays. From 1894 until the closure of the Woodham Ferrers – Maldon line to passengers on 10th September 1939, the route could still be used by passengers, but only by changing at Wickford, Woodham Ferrers, Maldon East and Witham. By this route the journey time for the 45 miles was three hours, whereas a journey between the two towns via Shenfield could take only two hours and two minutes although the distance was 52 3/4 miles.

A vintage scene at Woodham Ferris: the stationmaster is giving the 'right away' to the inattentive crew of Class M15 2-4-2T No.671   P.Lacey collection

The GER was most keen to build up residential business traffic at this time, particularly where the new lines were concerned and in an endeavour to encourage people to settle in the area, the Company produced a booklet in which Wickford was reported as having houses that were "built well apart" and that "the fresh air of the Thames Estuary circulates freely" – despite the fact that Wickford lies upon the upper reaches of the River Crouch and that the Thames is some miles away. Undoubtedly the coming of the railway caused the village to grow quite rapidly and a market was opened there in 1900. Cheap tickets to resorts and country towns were vigorously promoted in this period and, in 1901, a return ticket from London to Burnham on Crouch was advertised at the price of 8s 8d (43p) First Class and 4s 4d (22p) Third Class; fortnightly and weekend tickets were even cheaper.

At Southminster, horse sales took place monthly for nine months of the year, the exception being 'the Christmas and harvest months'. After each sale horse specials left the station, one being a through train to London, the other being a 'shorts' (stopping at various places along the line). Cattle sales were held weekly at the same location and after them trains of ten or twelve cattle wagons left the station.

There would appear to be some deficiencies in the standard of the buildings: just ten years after opening, in July 1899, the GER Way and Works

Committee authorised the expenditure of £623 on repairs and painting at Woodham Ferris, Burnham on Crouch and Southminster stations.

In the early years of the twentieth century, 'steam heated' carriages were a feature of the line during the winter months. A 200 gallon copper stood in the garden of Southminster station and was kept always on the boil. From this, heating cans were filled and placed in the compartments of passenger coaches – particularly those occupied by ladies – usually about sixteen cans per train. Southminster water was not popular with locomen however, as it caused locomotives to prime, making difficult starting for those stabled there overnight. Even at the end of the steam era, a blackboard could often be seen at Wickford, bearing the chalked message 'No water at Southminster'.

Although the route from Southend to Colchester had been so short-lived, a new proposal to link the two towns was put forward in November 1901. This was an amended version of a previous scheme to run an electric tramway from Southend to a pier at Bradwell on Sea, the route crossing the River Crouch at Creeksea and following the roads through Southminster and Tillingham to the shores of the Blackwater Estuary at a point just to the east of the hamlet of Bradwell Waterside. A map of the Blackwater end of the line shows the terminal station as being sited just inside the sea wall, with the pier extending out beyond the low water mark. Adjacent to the station an area is marked 'site of generating station', foreshadowing an event which was to occur on this same piece of land some sixty years later.

In June 1901 the scheme was notified to the Southend Corporation by a newly formed company known as The Railways and General Construction and Maintenance Company Ltd who said that they were applying at the next Parliamentary session for a Light Railway Order to build a line from Southend to Burnham on Crouch and Bradwell on Sea. As the southern part of the line would be within borough of Southend, they wanted to know what the Corporation's attitude would be towards the proposal, to which the Corporation replied that they would oppose any application for powers to operate independent tramways within the borough. In fact, the Southend tramway system was opened for traffic on 19th July 1901 and was built to a gauge of 3' 6", whereas the Company proposed to build their line to the standard gauge of 4' 8½". Even if the lines had operated with a gauge common to both the tramway and the Great Eastern branch, it was unlikely that the GER locomotives could have negotiated the sharp curves of the proposed tramway unless very short wheelbase locomotives such as the GER steam tram locomotives had been used, and it is unlikely that through working between the two systems would have materialised.

However, this was only the first proposal and, undaunted by the non-acceptance of their original scheme, the Company, in November 1901, deposited with the Light Railways Commission a further application for a Light Railway Order in respect of a line from Southend to Colchester, which crossed the Blackwater Estuary between Bradwell Waterside and Mersea Island, the route passing clear of the various villages instead of following the roads. Again, it was to have entered the Dengie Hundred by means of a bridge over the River Crouch at Creeksea, then run close to the Southminster branch in the vicinity of Burnham station and on to a junction, near Asheldham, with a northward extension of the GER line from Southminster.

When the Company's application was heard before the Light Railway Commissioners, the Corporation opposed the granting of powers for any running rights and also to the construction of the line southwards from Rochford to Southend, stating that they themselves were about to apply for such powers. The Commissioners found the Company's proposals unsatisfactory and refused to grant an order until more evidence could be produced as to the desirability and practicability of building the line.

Had the line been built, it would certainly have been a most interesting route and one can only speculate as to what type of bridge would have been built across the Blackwater Estuary. Presumably there would have been a lifting section or a swing bridge in the centre, or the River Blackwater would have been sealed to all but the smallest of shipping.

In October 1914, the GER 'Radical Alterations' timetable was introduced and the service reached its peak with 35 trains in each direction on the Southend line, ten on the Southminster and five on the Maldon branches on weekdays, with ten each way on the Southend line and three on the Southminster branch on Sundays.

However, war had broken out in August 1914 and these services had, before long, to be drastically reduced and decelerated although, with the threat of a German invasion, the east coast became a defence area and many special trains were run in connection with the coastal defences and the movement of troops. As the war went on many railwaymen enlisted and the remaining staff, with extra military trains and personnel shortages, were hard put to keep things going. Troop trains to the defences in the Dengie Peninsular were preceded at Southminster and other stations by a Railway Transport Officer, usually of the rank of Major, and this individual was explicit as to how and where the troop trains were to be distributed about the station yards. These trains often consisted of up to ten coaches and must have been some of the heaviest passenger trains ever seen upon the branch. There were eventually fifteen anti-aircraft guns sited upon the marshes to the east of Southminster, so troop trains and trains of military supplies were frequent arrivals at the terminus.

The staunch efforts of the GER staff during the early period of the war were recognised by the management with the following announcement which appeared in the 'Great Eastern Railway Magazine' for December 1914:

> "The Chief Traffic Manager desires to place on record his appreciation and thanks to all concerned in connection with the working of troop trains during the past few weeks. The duties undertaken in many cases involved arduous work and long hours, but in every case were performed in a spirit of loyalty and devotion which is to be much commended".

Excursion trains ran on to the branch regularly prior to the First World War: J15 649 is shown on one such train, the 2.15pm North Woolwich to Southminster, near Brentwood on 25th June 1908 (LCGB Ken Nunn Collection)

Air raids upon Britain, by Zeppelin airships, began in 1915, followed from 1917 onwards by raids by both airships and aeroplanes, with London as the main target. From their bases in Belgium, the usual route for the raiders was over the Essex coast where the Rivers Thames, Crouch and Blackwater, together with the GER main line, showed clearly the way to London, even at night. With railways a legitimate target, the GER was in the forefront of the battle and instructions were issued from Liverpool Street to all stations as to staff behaviour during air raids. The Southminster branch, the Maldon branches and the Southend line all came into GER Area No. 42, and this was the area used as an example in the issued instructions. For instance, the specimen air raid warning issued by the Liverpool Street Telegraph Office was 'P.A. Probable 42', which was, to save telegraph time, the code for 'Air Raid probable, Area No.42'. Similarly, 'S.P. Clear 42' was the code for 'All Clear, Area No.42'.

Station Masters, Inspectors and others were instructed to report immediately to the Chief Traffic Manager the presence and movement of hostile aircraft under the prefix 'P.A.', giving as far as possible the following information:

1. Number of aircraft
2. Whether aeroplane or airship
3. Time of observation
4. Direction in which the aircraft was seemingly proceeding
5. If bombs dropped

This would seem to be rather a lot to transmit over the telegraph but aircraft speeds then were relatively slow and the control room at Liverpool Street would be forewarned as to where trouble could be expected.

The two examples quoted in the instructions are worthy of note:

Example 1: suppose three hostile aeroplanes passed over Althorne at 11.30 am, and they were travelling towards Fambridge without dropping bombs, the message should be as follows:

'Three planes, eleven thirty am, west'.

Example 2: suppose five hostile aeroplanes and two hostile airships passed over Burnham on Crouch at 3pm travelling towards Maldon and bombs dropped, the message should be as follows:

'Five planes, two ships, three pm, north east, bombs dropped'.

From these examples, it is obvious that the Company expected trouble in the area and, in fact, a Zeppelin did drop bombs near the railway at Maldon and a Gotha was shot down at the mouth of the River Crouch. When an air raid was imminent, down trains were required to pull up at the next available station platform in order to allow the passengers to alight if they so wished, and were not permitted to proceed from the platform except for allowing a following train to enter the station in order to discharge its passengers. This must have been trying work for the signalmen concerned, but in wartime exceptions were made to normal procedure and the staff took it all in their stride.

In 1918, at the end of the war, the country's rail system was sadly run down after four years of poor maintenance, and many of the skilled staff who had enlisted so eagerly in the early days had left their bones under foreign soil. Female staff were employed during the war years to fill the gaps caused by men leaving to fight. Southminster had two lady porters, one of them being Lizzie King – doubtless related to both Joe and Harry King, who were also employed there. Most female staff had their employment terminated in 1921. Also, growing competition by road transport was a threat to revenue. Nevertheless, the peace time service on the Southminster branch was gradually restored, but it was never to surpass the 1914 standard of speed.

However, the future could only look better after the rigours of the war and in 1919 there were proposals for several new light railways in Essex. The 'Essex Chronicle' reported:

'There is probably no county better adapted than Essex for light railway extensions, there being no excessive gradients, expensive embankments, numerous bridges to be provided; and the following schemes are proposed as representing the minimum requirements of the county. Steam tramways upon roads have been suggested in lieu of light railways of the ordinary gauge to avoid transhipment, and also capable of taking passenger traffic, but the Highways and Transport Sub-Committee are of the opinion that light railways are preferable'.

No less than eight proposals were put forward, Number 5 on the list being for a line which 'would commence at the GER terminus at Southminster and proceed northward via Tillingham to Bradwell on Sea, a distance of six miles. This line would tap a milk, seed and wheat growing district. Its construction would stimulate the production of milk, seeds and potatoes'.

Once again an extension of the line to Bradwell had been suggested and once again nothing came of the scheme.

In 1923 there occurred what many consider the first step towards the nationalisation of British railways - The Grouping. The Great Eastern Railway became a part of the London and North Eastern Railway Company although, apart from a change of initials on railway equipment and uniforms etc little difference was noticeable. The same locomotives pulled the same coaches, the stations looked as before and the Great Eastern atmosphere still existed, particularly on the rural branch lines. Train services on the Southminster branch never again regained the 1914 intensity, the LNER seeming content with things as they stood.

In February 1925 the subject of the Southend to Colchester line arose once more after many years of silence. The Southend and Colchester Light Railway Company announced that it was seeking authority to revive its powers, which had by then lapsed, to construct the lines covered by its Acts, but Southend Corporation were experimenting with trolleybuses at their end of the proposed route and were not really interested. The Corporation decided to wait and see whether the Company made any real progress, but heard nothing further and the proposed link at Southminster remained a dream.

A trace of this dream remains on Mersea Island to this day, for at West Mersea, Fairhaven Avenue runs in a straight line from the beach into the island and just beyond the crossroads with East Road would have been the site of the station. On some old maps Fairhaven Avenue is shown as Station Road.

N7 69620 approaching Woodham from Southminster 17th September 1956 (Frank Church, courtesy of the Essex Bus Enthusiasts Group)

There were few alterations to the Southminster branch during the interwar depression years, although even during those days there were special excursion trains, of up to eight coaches, to Burnham on Crouch, which was growing in popularity with visitors who preferred something quieter than the noisy brashness of Southend. Yachting activities at Burnham, and to a lesser extent at Fambridge, Althorne and South Woodham Ferrers, were on the increase up to 1939, many yachtsmen reaching their craft by way of the branch line, although travel by motor car was rapidly increasing in popularity. This maritime aspect of the branch was always present, particularly at weekends when Friday evenings saw passengers in yachting gear and carrying duffle bags arriving for a weekend of sailing or working upon their boats, whilst Sunday evening trains carried them back to the confines of the city from the wide skies and salt water. Guards on the line carried in their vans strange packages – oozing canvas bags and shiny tins pierced with many holes, the former holding oysters from the Crouch, the latter containing maggots for inland angling clubs.

During the 1930s, the Woodham Ferrers station staff were kept busy when the hunt held their meet on the forecourt of the adjoining Station Hotel, now the Ferris Arms, and five or six horse wagons would arrive in the station goods yard, each containing two or three horses.

But shadows were looming over Europe and those halcyon days would soon be but a memory. The last peacetime service on the branch consisted of nine trains each way, plus an additional down train on Thursdays only which connected at Wickford with the midnight train from Liverpool Street. On Saturdays there were thirteen trains each way, whilst on Sundays there were but two trains each way. The only through London train left Southminster at 8.18 am, arriving at Liverpool Street at 9.50 am, and returning at 1.27 pm (2.40 pm on Saturdays). On Mondays to Fridays these trains called only at Billericay, Wickford and Burnham on Crouch, reaching Southminster at 2.53 pm.

In September 1939, following the declaration of war, all railways in Britain were placed upon an emergency footing and passenger services became subject to delays and reductions as priority was given to troop trains and trains of strategic materials. Staff shortages arose as personnel left the railways to join the armed forces and many women were employed in railway service to fill the gaps. An early wartime casualty was the passenger service between Woodham Ferrers and Maldon, which ceased on 10th September 1939, never to be resumed, although goods traffic continued.

Prior to the fall of France in the early summer of 1940 and the resulting change of the strategic situation, the east coast was considered to be one of the most 'sensitive' areas of the country and Essex was expected to receive a large share of enemy attention, perhaps even to be invaded. Accordingly, thousands of troops were drafted into the area to guard the coastline, particularly the estuaries by way of which an invader could penetrate into the heart of the county. Many Royal Marines were stationed in Burnham on Crouch and other riverside locations, and troop trains were frequently to be seen travelling the Southminster branch.

Notwithstanding the enemy threat to the area, train loads of evacuees came from London, depositing their cargoes of awe-stricken humanity upon the station platforms along the line, where they gazed horrified and aghast at the emptiness of a countryside which many of them had never before seen. As the last puffs of smoke from the receding train drifted away in the distance, their feeling of abandonment was complete.

Enemy air activity over the Dengie Peninsular, quite heavy even in the early days of the war, intensified during the Battle of Britain and attacks by low flying aircraft became a new hazard. During the course of one such incident a lady booking clerk from Southminster station was shot in the arm, and in another a parachute mine came to earth and exploded behind the houses in Station Road, Southminster. In all, there were 326 air raid warnings in the area in 1940 alone. Needless to say, those evacuees who had not already returned home were sent away to safer areas and the branch line was their escape route from both the bombing and the unfamiliar countryside.

At Bradwell, the pre-war refuelling landing ground, which had been built to serve the nearby bombing and gunnery range on the Dengie Flats, was developed into an operational airfield, commencing operations on 28th November 1941. The conveyance of materials for the enlargement of the airfield made plenty of work for the branch line and Southminster station yard saw much coming and going as RAF lorries picked up goods from the railway and 'liberty buses' came and went with service personnel proceeding to and from leave. Amongst the extra traffic for the airfield were train loads of petrol, which was used for fog dispersal.

This was a busy and trying time for the branch line staff, coping with extra traffic, suffering the irksome wartime restrictions, the blackout and the air raids. The proximity to Southminster of such an important airfield and its attraction to enemy intruder aircraft put the station in the forefront of the battle zone and many of the staff – as they were all along the line – were members of the Air Raid Precautions services and the Home Guard. They carried out their duties with admirable devotion despite the difficulties and a typical example is that of the railwayman who, each morning, walked the track from his home at Fambridge to man the first train out of Wickford. This was a walk of eight miles and must have been an ordeal in the bleak, black hours of a bitter winter morning, but it had to be done and so was done.

The hazard and strain experienced by the railway workers of the Southminster branch will be apparent from the fact that during the period of hostilities, what was known as the eastern area of Essex – that is the Boroughs of Maldon and Burnham and Maldon Rural District received:

26778 explosive and incendiary bombs
83 parachute mines
83 V1 flying bombs
54 V2 rockets
25 persons killed and 191 injured

Several of the V1's came to earth in the area of the Southminster line and a V2 fell at Fambridge, several more exploding in the air above the line. A V1 bomb in 1944 destroyed the Railway Cottages at Battlesbridge, thankfully without casualties.

The railwaymen and women can indeed be proud of the way in which they carried out their duties of moving trains of civilians and troops, plus goods trains of vital agricultural and military materials under such trying circumstances.

Chapter 4: Life On The Line: The Later Years

The end of the Second World War again found the railways in a rundown condition, with a backlog of maintenance work, worn out stock and with the threat of increased road competition. The scene on the Southminster branch still resembled days past as trains of wooden coaches hauled by locomotives of GER origin made their leisurely way across the marshes and fields.

Bradwell Bay airfield closed to flying in 1946, all that remained being a small contingent of American airmen who occupied some buildings and kept a fast range launch at Bradwell Waterside. It was proposed that the airfield should be developed into a civil airport, particularly as it was one of fifteen U.K. airfields equipped with fog dispersal apparatus, but one of the factors which ruled out the idea was that the Southminster branch did not extend to Bradwell on Sea. It is therefore interesting to conjecture what would have happened to the Dengie Peninsular had the proposed Southend to Colchester line become a reality.

Just after the war an unusual accident happened at Woodham Ferrers on a bleak Sunday afternoon at dusk and in a heavy snowstorm. A rake of wagons was left on the Southminster line, just beyond the crossing and the junction points, while the locomotive propelled another rake, some forty in number, a short distance and on a rising gradient, along the Maldon line. On the footplate were the driver, fireman, guard and stationmaster. The wagon brakes were pinned down at the parking place, the locomotive uncoupling and returning, coming to a stand beyond the junction points and near to the level crossing. The points were changed and the locomotive was just moving back to pick up the first rake of wagons, when out of the snow rumbled the forty wagons at an ever increasing speed - presumably the brakes had not been properly pinned down. There was an immediate split second conference among those on the footplate and all decided to stay with the engine. The ensuing impact was violent and shattering, the tender of the locomotive took the full force and weight of the runaway wagons, and being split in the process lost all its water, some of which put out the locomotive's fire.

In the station premises, the stationmaster's wife and son heard the crash and rushed outside to see what had happened, but their gaze revealed only a vast cloud of steam beyond the crossing. As the steam subsided everyone took a look at this scene of devastation and were struck by the fact that in the wreckage were several pairs of wagon wheels and it was thought that they must have been part of a wagon load. Later it was realised that they were parts of three wagons which had totally disintegrated, being identifiable only by their number plates which were found in various places. Undoubtedly, the decision of the crew to stay on the footplate saved their lives as the entire area was littered with fragments of the wrecked wagons which would have scythed down anyone unfortunate enough to have been in their way.

As there was still the Sunday evening passenger train to come, a bus was procured to bridge the gap between Woodham Ferrers and Fambridge, but the driver had no idea of the route, the darkness was by then complete and the snow falling even faster. The stationmaster's teenage son volunteered to act as pilot to the bus driver and the ensuing drive was hazardous in the extreme. The road was then narrower than it is today, with a steep hill and many bends to negotiate, the bus slipped and slid its way to Fambridge, whereupon the driver indicated in no uncertain terms that this was to be his sole trip and set off upon the return journey, dropped the stationmaster's son at the top of the road to Woodham Ferrers station and disappeared into the blizzard.

2 car DMU at Althorne on 17th October 1956
(Frank Church, courtesy of the Essex Bus Enthusiasts Group)

In the same area, another accident at Woodham Ferrers resulted in a fatality. Fenn Crossing lies to the west of the station and was equipped with gates of the manual type. Intending to drive across the track to the houses on the far side, a local motorist opened the first gate and then, contrary to the usual instructions, drove his Ford Prefect onto the line without having also opened the far gate. Before he could get out of his car to do so, a steam hauled goods train ran into the car and, with the unfortunate motorist trapped inside; the vehicle was reduced to crumpled scrap as it was propelled almost into Woodham Ferrers yard before the train could be brought to a halt. Unfortunately there were to be several similar accidents in subsequent years.

Nationalisation, the final act of the process set in motion with the 1923 Grouping and delayed in execution by the war years, took place in 1948 and the Southminster branch became part of the Eastern Region of British Railways. At last the aged rolling stock was due for retirement as steam working was to be abandoned. The locomotives were showing their age and at Althorne, one freezing winter morning, the train to Wickford gave up the ghost, a thin plume of smoke from the cutting half a mile east of the station marking the spot at which the venerable loco had ground to a halt. Althorne station's lady porter, Miss Dorothy Palmer, set off along the track, returning some thirty minutes later with a 'refugee column' of disgruntled passengers, complete with guard, far from happy after their stumbling walk along the icy sleepers to the station. The failed locomotive was towed back to Burnham on Crouch, another substituted, and the passengers resumed their journey, albeit somewhat late. By 1950 the locomotive shed at Southminster had lost its roof.

During the twilight of steam on the branch, sugar beet trains left Burnham yard at 6pm each night during the season and a Burnham resident, then a schoolboy, recalls how he would visit the yard after school each day, cultivating a friendship with the loco crew, until a trip on the footplate as the train was made up, became his daily treat. Also at this time, Roberts Brothers circus visited Burnham each year and an unusual sight at the end of their stay was the loading of elephants from the cattle dock. At Althorne, a regular traveller, who worked as a night watchman in London, left his dog at the station each night to await his master's return in the morning. As the oil lamps flickered along the platform and as the evening train pulled in, the dog would appear in the hopes that one of the alighting passengers would turn out to be his master.

Cattle would, and still do, sometimes stray onto the line, and if the guard was unable to shift them, a weary search would begin for the farmer concerned who, often as not, turned out to be the tiny figure on the sea wall. Whilst the loco simmered amidst the cattle as they browsed upon the lush grass at the trackside, the passengers would fret at the delay, their chances of making the connection at Wickford becoming less and less as the time ticked by.

On the subject of livestock, in 1954 a Tillingham farmer had 500 sheep brought from Scotland to Southminster station by train. From thence they were driven to Tillingham and, in his opinion, this was a fine way of transporting animals to various parts of the country, but this traffic was discontinued throughout British Rail from 1st January 1963. The same person also recalled that at this time a telephone call to London in the morning would result in the delivery of a parcel to stations on the line by the same evening, but parcels were later only sent as far as Wickford and collected from there, so the use of this service declined as a result. In the early 1990s this service was discontinued.

An unusual incident took place in the early 1950s when two local residents out fishing from their launch in the River Crouch, spotted what appeared to be a very large box or container floating low in the water. When they pulled alongside the object they found it to be an ancient railway box wagon with only six inches or so of its top parts showing above the surface. Securing a line to it, they towed the wagon to the River Roach where, as it drew so much water it grounded long before the launch. Here it was left until the next high tide and was then towed to Paglesham where greased boards had been prepared in order to slide the vehicle onto the saltings. This accomplished, the wagon became a boat gear store and still sits there to this day. The wagon appears to be some sort of parcels or utility van and is very old, judging by its shape and construction. The two metal discs which remained upon it, and which bore the words 'Tare 13 tons', were presented to the Stour Valley Railway Preservation Society (now the East Anglian Railway Museum) for display in their museum at Chappel and Wakes Colne station.

There was a character and friendliness on the Southminster line, guards would hold trains as they waited for tardy passengers and even in diesel days would

2 car DMU at Woodham Ferrers on 17th September 1956
(Frank Church, courtesy of the Essex Bus Enthusiasts Group)

sometimes set back into the platform to pick up latecomers. A good example of this friendliness and as a last glimpse of steam days, the experience of a yachtsman who arrived hot and exhausted at Burnham station one Monday morning only to see his train disappearing into the distance under a cloud of white smoke, may sum up all that was best on a rural branch line. The thwarted traveller needed urgently to reach London and, having just missed the 9 am train, was dismayed to find that the next passenger train was two hours hence. However, the obliging booking clerk suggested that he went to the yard where a goods train for Wickford was shortly to leave, and to have a word with the guard as to what could be done.

In the yard the yachtsman found a train consisting of an elderly locomotive, two wagons and a brake van. The guard was most friendly and assured him they would get him to Wickford in time to make his connection and that while he was purchasing his ticket he, the guard, would confer with the driver and would also telephone to the stations on the line to ask the staff to be ready to speed up the shunting operations which had to be carried out. Within five minutes the train had left Burnham with the yachtsman seated in the brake van where, having remarked that he had left his boat in too much of a hurry for breakfast, he was offered a share of the guard's sandwiches. This offer he felt bound to decline, but with grateful thanks.

Shunting operations were carried out at both Woodham Ferrers and Battlesbridge with unprecedented alacrity and the train arrived at Wickford in what must have been a record time for the trip. Thanks and a token of appreciation were offered to the loco crew and the guard, who accepted with some diffidence, and the passenger felt that he now knew how it was to be a VIP! His first reaction was to write to BR a letter of appreciation regarding the service rendered, but then he was struck by with the thought that the guard had broken every rule in the book and that a discreet silence would be the best thing for all concerned. A charming picture from the not so distant past and an episode probably far from unique upon rural branch lines.

Mr. J. Ford recalls that on one occasion when he lived at Battlesbridge his father fell asleep and was over-carried to Woodham Ferrers. When he explained his plight to one of the station staff he was put aboard a light engine complete with his baggage and conveyed back to Battlesbridge, where he was put down adjacent to his house accompanied by a blast on the whistle. Service indeed – albeit highly unofficial!

At the end of steam services the branch had a service of eleven down and twelve up trains on weekdays, with an additional train in each direction on Saturdays, whilst on Sundays there were still only two trains in each direction. Freight services were two trains each way Mondays to Fridays and one on Saturdays, with the Monday to Friday afternoon train calling at Hogwell siding as required. By summer 1954 Hogwell and Creeksea sidings had closed, but there was a new siding serving Parr's works on the outskirts of Wickford: this utilised part of the erstwhile Fanton Curve from Belchamps Junction. This siding was served by a trip from Wickford that continued to Battlesbridge. Shunting at Burnham on Crouch yard, together with the working of the quarry and engineer's sidings between Southminster and Burnham, was done by the Southminster pilot locomotive. By the same date, both Battlesbridge and Althorne signalboxes opened only for freight movements, and by 1961 Battlesbridge had been converted to a ground frame.

Services by diesel unit commenced on 11th June 1956 and the travelling times were reduced: however, the one remaining through train to London was withdrawn at this time. The diesel sets seemed strange to passengers used to the narrow, small windowed compartments of the old carriages as the view was much wider and they were able to look along the track both from front and rear. The new service also provided a greater frequency than before, especially on Sundays, an interesting working on that day being the 6.50 am train from Stratford to Southminster, calling at Romford, Shenfield and all stations hence. Improved connections to and from London followed the introduction of electric services to Southend from 31 December 1956. Steam hauled goods services lingered on for a while longer, but soon they too were replaced by diesels.

An event of great importance to the Southminster branch occurred in the following year, the laying of the foundation stone of one of Britain's first three nuclear powered electricity generating stations on the old airfield at Bradwell on Sea. In fact the site covered the area shown on the 1912 maps of the proposed tramway from Southend to Bradwell on Sea as 'site for generating station'. Once

The trial ACV lightweight railcar was tested on the branch, and is seen here at Southminster in September 1953 (Frank Church, courtesy Essex Bus Enthusiasts Group)

more gangs of construction workers were seen in the Dengie Hundred and it was said that on pay nights the scenes in many villages were akin to those in old western movies! The building of such a vast complex meant work for the railway line and during this period station yards along the branch were host to piles of materials used in the construction of one of the main pylon runs which followed almost the same route. The grand opening ceremony at the generating station took place in 1962, many of the visiting VIP's present arriving at Southminster station aboard a special train reputedly equipped with Pullman carriages.

In Southminster station yard a large gantry appeared, its purpose being to transfer on to special railway trucks the huge concrete nuclear waste flasks brought by lorry from the generating station and destined for treatment in the north of England. How much simpler the task would have been had the line been extended as far as Bradwell in 1889! To the railwaymen, the nuclear waste trains became known as 'bomb trains' and the flasks as 'coffins'. Most of them were not much worried about this traffic, but it is on record that one signalman would put himself on the floor when a nuclear waste train passed his box in order to avoid being 'impregnated'! It should be mentioned that, although this behaviour may have seemed a little eccentric, this signalman was another with a marked sense of duty, cycling each day – in all weathers – from Canvey Island to Wickford whence he travelled by train to his place of work.

Plans were drawn up in 1958 for the rationalisation of facilities at Southminster, to include demolition of the remains of the engine shed, the infilling

Class 37 hauled nuclear waste train passing Battlesbridge in 1970 (Paddy Lacey)

of the ash pits, and the removal of the turntable and coal stage: it is believed that this work was carried out in the same year.

While all the excitement of building and opening the nuclear generating station had been taking place at one end of the line, at the other end the goods traffic from Woodham Ferrers to Maldon quietly ceased on 31st June 1959, the track being lifted during the following year. Thus Woodham Ferrers ceased to be a junction station. Goods facilities were withdrawn from Althorne on 19th December 1960 and the loop there was subsequently removed. Goods trains of the conventional type were getting fewer and fewer during the late 1950s and early 1960s, but gravel trains were regularly using the branch, carrying loads from the large pits near Southminster station – these were initially hauled by Class 15 locomotives and loaded to a maximum of 450 tons. There were, of course, the regular nuclear waste trains, many of them being moved by night, which entailed extra work for railway staff. Public road transport in the area was still poor and at a meeting of a local parish committee, complaints were made about the charging of parking fees at stations along the line. It was claimed that British Railways were cashing in on the situation and a speaker said "it is rubbing in salt, having to pay parking fees in addition to the inflated railway fares". There had been some housing development at several places near the railway and the number of commuters was growing. The introduction of parking fees was an unpopular innovation.

The Beeching 'Axe' was by now hanging over the British railway system and, as branch lines appeared to be the main target, concern was felt for the future of the Southminster line. In August 1962, the local newspaper voiced this concern in an article headed "Will we lose our rail services? Maldon and Burnham may lose branch lines". The doubts remained unresolved and in January 1963 Burnham Council were invited to become corporate members of the Society for the Reinvigoration of Unremunerative Branch Railway Lines in The United Kingdom, which invitation was considered and deferred by their General Purposes Committee.

On the operating side, January 1963 saw some of the worst blizzards ever all over Britain, the whole country being held in winter's icy grip for several months thereafter, and on the Southminster line a diesel passenger set was caught in a drift between Wickford and Battlesbridge, the line being completely blocked until the train could be dug out. Nevertheless, the railways were able to keep to their schedules far better than road transport during this period, emphasising the benefits of retaining a railway in rural areas.

Possible closure of the line was again a topic when Burnham Council General Purposes Committee met in May 1963, Councillor John Dowding stating his belief that the Council should take up the offer made by the S.F.T.R.O.U.B.R.L.I.T.U.K He produced a copy of the Beeching Plan, which contained no mention of a closure of the Southminster branch, and said "I believe that this recommendation was made on the assumption that the Beeching Report was out and that we are not mentioned in it and, therefore, we are alright". Councillor Dowding considered this to be a parochial view and state "We are not, in fact, alright", going on to say that the branch carried 7000 passengers per week, but needed 10000 per week to break even. If the ballast workings were to cease he said that he believed that the line would be under threat. Other councillors suggested that they should have their own organisation rather than take up the proposed corporate membership, but this does not seem to have been taken further.

Some smaller matters were raising adverse comment amongst the line's passengers at this time. In the summer of 1963 an eight minute change in the timing of the first morning train to Wickford resulted in a petition to the Traffic Manager as it was felt that the retiming would make many commuters late for work. Later in the same year, Althorne Parish Council complained about the state of the road to the station which, they claimed, was full of potholes. Being at the end of a long lane, Althorne station could be a lonely place when things were quiet and Miss Palmer, now stationmaster, on duty alone one lunchtime was not happy to see arrive out of the blue a man obviously very much the worse for drink. No trains were due for some time, so she wondered what his purpose there could be. The conversation was brief:

Miss Palmer: "What do you want?"

Drunk: "Actually, I've come to rape you"

Miss Palmer: "That will make a change!"

Exit drunk, muttering, and it is hoped that the long climb back up the lane helped to restore him to some degree of sobriety!

Althorne in June 1960 (Douglas Thompson, EARM collection)

The school summer holidays of 1964 brought a number of cases of vandalism to the line and in early August an afternoon train was brought to a halt near Battlesbridge because youths had removed rail chairs from a platelayer's hut and placed them upon the track. The fuel tanks of the train were punctured by pieces of metal and many gallons of fuel oil were lost, the train having to be withdrawn and a replacement provided. A BR spokesman said that there had been a considerable number of similar incidents on the line since the commencement of the holidays.

The nearby Witham to Maldon branch was closed to passengers on 7th September 1964, and in 1965 fears again arose for the future of the Southminster line. The goods sidings were all closed from 4th October 1965, leaving just the aggregate and nuclear waste traffic from Southminster, and the last passenger train each weekday evening was cut out of the timetable, the passengers feeling that these actions would be the beginning of the end. By this time the Crouch Valley Railway Users Association was in being and a campaign was launched in an endeavour to save the line, the Burnham Week yachting regatta being one of the events liable, in their opinion, to die out if closure took place. The evening train which had been deleted was the 10.18pm Wickford to Southminster, and its going effectively ruined the chances of rail passengers having an evening out in London, as the last connecting train from Liverpool Street now left at 8.24pm. The last buses ran even earlier and a North Fambridge resident complained that British Railways was "pushing the Dengie Hundred back into the dark ages".

The C.V.R.U.A. felt that BR was liable to economise itself out of existence and suggested savings such as continental level crossings to save labour costs, and reduced rate return tickets to attract yachtsmen. They also felt that railway publicity could have been more imaginative and effective, avoiding the type of thing which had recently occurred when Burnham on Crouch had been billed as Burnham on Sea, which is of course in Somerset.

British Railways did not refute any of the prophecies of closure which were made at the time and so the worries about it continued to multiply. However, some people felt that these fears were groundless, for at Burnham on Crouch the British Transport Yacht Club had taken over the down platform ladies' waiting room for their own use and it was felt that the line would stay open – at least as far as Burnham – if only for the convenience of the club, despite the inconvenience to lady passengers! No-one at Burnham station seemed to know from whence the yacht club came, or how often. At irregular intervals a face would appear at the booking office window and a request was made for the key, which was handed over with no questions asked. Burnham station must have been unique in having, whilst still open for business, a yacht club on its platform and the only one in Essex where it was possible to step straight from train to clubhouse! (The yacht club at Leigh on Sea took up residence in the old Leigh on Sea station only after it was replaced by a new station some distance westwards).

On 24th February 1965 the branch actually saw its first electric train, albeit unplanned and without the benefit of overhead wires! Following problems with the point locking in Wickford signalbox, an eight car train bound for Southend passed over the affected points. The front unit and the first bogie of the front car of the second unit carried on to Southend as planned, but the remaining cars went on to the Southminster line. For around a quarter of a mile there was no problem as the lines are parallel: however the branch then curves to the north and the fifth car struck the fortunately empty platelayers hut in the 'V' between the two lines and became derailed.

1967 saw the first of a series of derailments which plagued the line for some years when, on 8th August, seven ballast wagons left the rails at Althorne station, partly demolishing the platform and covering it ankle deep in sand and stones. The locomotive and eleven other wagons travelled over half a mile before coming to a halt. The guard escaped with bruises and a porter and passenger escaped unhurt despite their being showered with stones as they stood upon the platform. The train was travelling towards Southminster and about half a mile of track was wrecked but the line was back in use within four days, a special bus service being put on during that time for Southminster, Burnham and Althorne rail users.

British Railways officials seemed unable to give a reason for the derailment; although poor track maintenance could have been a cause. A farmer at Fambridge claimed in the same month that the track near his home was being undermined by the tide and that sleepers and chairs had broken away leaving the rails 'flapping in the air'. This was denied by a spokesman from BR, who said "there is no danger to passengers. We obviously would not run trains over lines which were unsafe or suspended". He went on to state that routine maintenance was always being carried out on the line and if the track was sinking it was by so little that nothing more than that was called for. The farmer, however, maintained that trains passing at 60mph within a few feet of his house lurched and were in danger of smashing into his residence. Following the closure of Battlesbridge loop on 7th December 1966, the loops and signalboxes at Woodham Ferrers, Burnham on Crouch and Althorne all closed on 21st January 1967.

In 1967 the aggregate trains from Southminster to Mile End began to be hauled by more powerful Class 37 locomotives, with the resultant loadings increasing to 550 tons.

Later in the same year, BR issued a statement saying that they were to carry out demolitions at stations along the whole length of the line as part of a drive to cut costs. If the demolitions were not carried out, they claimed, they would be faced with enormous bills for dry rot and external repairs, the costs of which could never be met by revenue from the passenger service. Most stations were to have buildings demolished, those at Battlesbridge station facing the most drastic of all, and even the passenger toilet facilities were to disappear, BR claiming that they 'were conforming with national policy'. An editorial in the local newspaper said that there had been nothing but decline along the line in the past ten years and that train services had deteriorated to such an extent that if the latest plans were extended it would be 'like taking a slow ride across the desert'. Many saw it as part of a plot to bring about closure of the line, but there were others who realised that only by drastic savings in staff and facilities could the line survive.

So, in the spring of 1968, down came most of the buildings and the Old Great Eastern image was banished for good. The station sidings had already gone, the only two signal boxes remaining were those at Fambridge and Southminster, but there was no increase in passenger services. The twenty-five members of the British Transport Yacht Club moved into a building on the up side of Burnham station when their ex-ladies waiting room on the down side was demolished, but the station toilet block was saved from demolition by the Council agreeing to take it over at a cost of £205 per annum (£5 rent and £200 service charge). The tenancy had been offered by BR, but some members of the Council thought it a hard bargain.

Another case of vandalism occurred on 22nd August 1968, when children placed a heap of scrap metal on to the rails near Burnham station. The train was carrying between thirty and forty commuters and had just reached a speed of 30 mph after leaving the station, when the driver saw the obstruction and applied the brakes, but the train hit the heap of metal and came to a halt just beyond. The driver and guard then loaded the metal on to the train for inspection at Southminster by the police. Only a few weeks earlier a group of boys had pushed a pile of gravel from a Burnham bridge into the path of a train and, after the second incident, Mr Wilfred Lord, stationmaster at Wickford, appealed to parents to control their children "not

Through diesel train from Liverpool Street to Southminster on 17th August 1957 shortly after departing Wickford, formed of two two-car Wickham lightweight units (Frank Church, courtesy Essex Bus Enthusiasts Group)

on behalf of British Rail, but on behalf of common humanity". "One of these children is going to get killed one of these days" he said.

The following month saw another derailment. On 30th September three ballast wagons and a brake van left the rails at Battlesbridge, the guard breaking his collarbone in the accident, which happened just after midnight. The train was on its way from Southminster to Wickford and the wagons broke free when passing through the station, ripping up eighty yards of track in the process. Six buses and a taxi were laid on to carry rail passengers from villages between Battlesbridge and Southminster to Wickford and a BR spokesman said that an enquiry would be held, although the cause of the accident was not yet known. For some months afterwards passengers travelling on the restored track were treated to the dismal sight of smashed and overturned wagons strewn about the scene of the derailment.

Towards the end of the year, the then Minister of Transport, Mr Richard Marsh, revealed that a cash grant of £62 million was to be paid out to over 200 loss-making but socially desirable lines and that the Southminster line was to be one of the lucky recipients. The grant for 1969-70 was £106,000: that for 1971-2 was £101,000. Also came the news that there was the possibility of the line being taken over by the Greater London Passenger Transport Authority within two years, but nothing further was heard of this. Although the line was losing money overall, its freight services were making a profit. More and bigger freight trains were called for to carry the ballast from Southminster, notwithstanding that their numbers had increased from two to three per day. A BR spokesman said that the freight trains were maintaining the passenger service and that an extensive programme of relaying and track improvements was under way. Ultimately, he stated, the line was to be doubled and electrified, but the rumour that it was planned to run ballast trains at 90 mph on the improved track was an exaggeration!

1969 was a year of strife as far as the ever growing army of commuters using the branch was concerned. A storm of protest was unleashed when BR revealed early in January that there were to be no more Sunday trains: these were withdrawn from 12th January 1969. Everybody joined in the battle to restore the service – members of Parliament, local councils, residents associations, commuters, rail users associations and local residents themselves, to name but a few. Maldon's MP, Mr Brian Harrison, accused British Rail of trying to erode the service by making it uncomfortable and inconvenient, ten hoteliers and licensees in Burnham sent a combined letter of protest, villagers in South Woodham Ferrers presented a 251-signature petition and the local newspaper was inundated with anti-BR letters. In all, five Members of Parliament pledged their support for the campaign to the Crouch Rail Users' Association and all sorts of bodies swung into action against BR. The Southminster to Wickford Rail Users' Association attacked them for 'inadequate administration' and referred to late trains causing missed connections at Wickford, which, in turn, resulted in the line having a much larger deficit than necessary, whilst the Nursery Estate Residents Association at South Woodham Ferrers claimed that at least fifty per cent of the morning travellers from Woodham Ferrers did not pay for their tickets as the trains were so crowded that the guard found it impossible to travel from one end of the train to the other. British Rail's reply was that checks had been carried out at Wickford and that there was no large scale evasion of fares. Furthermore, they claimed that the income from Sunday train passengers did not cover the cost of crews and fuel and, in reply to MP Brian Harrison, they stated that they had no intention of restoring the service during the summer. For those without private transport the Dengie Hundred was indeed slipping 'back into the dark ages'.

In the midst of the arguments, claims and counterclaims, the North Fambridge farmer again complained that the stretch of line which ran across his land was threatened by high tides. He maintained that part of the railway embankment was acting as a sea wall and that it could be swept away should there be a big tidal surge. British Rail denied this and said that they would not contemplate running trains on tracks that were below the required standard.

Meanwhile, Burnham businessman Mr Edgar Samuel, publicly made known his intention to cause the 'biggest clobbering up of services BR's Eastern Region has seen' with a series of sit-downs on the main railway line between Wickford and

Fambridge looking east: two car Cravens unit forming the 1508 Wickford to Southminster on 4th September 1979 (G R Mortimer)

London. In a letter to the Transport Minister Mr Samuel warned that demonstrators would strike if the Sunday service between Wickford and Southminster was not restored. "We are completely cut off from civilisation on Sundays. The majority of residents are country folk and they cannot afford to run cars", he said.

On 12th February, Mr Samuel carried out his threat and staged a lone sit-down in front of an electric train on the main line at Wickford. He had travelled from Burnham by car, dressed in a sheepskin jacket, thick trousers, scarf and thick soled boots and, just after 8 a.m. crouched on the line in front of a Liverpool Street bound train, holding up its departure for four minutes. Before him Mr Samuel carried a poster bearing the inscription "Restore Burnham's Sunday Service". Needless to say, pictures of the event found their way into both the local and national newspapers and Mr Samuel was quoted as saying that the Sunday closure was 'bloody dreadful'. He said that other people had been prepared to sit on the line with him, but if they had done so, the protest would have turned into an 'L.S.E. rabble'. (L.S.E. – the London School of Economics – students had a reputation at this time for being very militant).

After the event, Mr Samuel was escorted by an official into an office where he said that he had not bought a platform ticket and was told that he would be reported for trespassing. He then had a cup of tea in a nearby café after which he returned to Burnham. British Rail's Liverpool Street divisional Public Relations Officer, Mr Percy Gillett, commented that Mr Samuel's action had not caused any disruption of train services, but that he had reported the matter to the police. "We feel that this was a foolhardy thing to do", he said. During the following week, both Mr Samuel and photographer Roger Nadal were interviewed by the British Transport Police, Mr Samuel at his home where he was cautioned and told that he would be reported for consideration of prosecution for trespassing and also causing an obstruction, and Mr Nadal at his place of work, where he was also cautioned and told he would be reported for consideration of prosecution for trespassing and also aiding and abetting Mr Samuel to cause an obstruction. Meanwhile, the Transport Police were trying to trace other photographers who took pictures of the incident.

Despite all this publicity the Sunday trains were not restored and one local resident was incensed when he saw bridge repairs being carried out, the working party being safeguarded by lookouts. "Nothing wrong with that!" he wrote to the press, "except that it was a Sunday and there were no trains – or was a Beeching ghost train scheduled to roar through on its way to Maldon East or Langford Halt!" He also went on to state that BR staff were still not collecting tickets along the line and that on one occasion, when travelling from Burnham during the week, he was unable to obtain a ticket from the guard, who referred him to Wickford station ticket office, which refused to issue one. This non-collection of tickets was seen by many people as a deliberate action in order to show low passenger usage of the line and thus justify closure. It was reputed to have happened on other branch lines just before they were closed.

In the following month the line was closed for a while between Althorne and Southminster after torrential rain caused a landslip near Althorne. While engineers were working to fill in the weakened embankment, 500 commuters a day were being carried by emergency bus services. Then in May came more fears that the Southminster line might be facing closure. A gravel firm wished to start a new pit at Ratsborough Farm, Southminster, and it was rumoured that if the county planning authorities turned down their application the firm might move out of the area when their present workings were exhausted, costing British Rail £400 per day in lost freight charges. By this time there were two ballast trains per day from Southminster, the loads being carried on to Mile End ballast depot where they were dropped into former coal staithes for onward delivery by road. With the line operating on such a delicate balance, the loss of this trade could well prove to be its downfall and the Crouch Valley Rail Users Association wrote to Maldon Rural District Council and the county planning department asking them to treat the gravel firm's application sympathetically in view of the danger to the line.

Undoubtedly the ballast trains helped to keep the Southminster line open, with 175,000 tons moved in 1969, but the nuclear waste trains must have been the prime reason for its survival, notwithstanding that the commuter traffic had increased greatly since the Second World War. The nuclear waste trains travelled to Temple Mills yard in East London, where locomotives were changed for the journey to the north. Travelling to Southminster, locomotives were allowed to run at up to 50mph but the nuclear waste trains to Temple Mills were limited to 25mph and no

DMU leaving Burnham bound for Southminster on 16th May 1967
(Dennis Swindale)

stopping was allowed at stations en route. When one did come to a halt at Fambridge station, an agitated signalman rushed to the train to tell the crew to move on. He had his instructions about keeping the nuclear waste trains moving, but unfortunately BR had omitted to issue such instructions to the loco crew!

When there were still sidings at stations along the branch, nuclear waste trains were often parked in them, which in the case of Woodham Ferrers meant quite near to the road and to houses. If parked overnight, a BR employee was supposed to guard the train and its deadly cargo all night, but one railwayman allocated to this duty at Althorne was heard to say "I wasn't going to hang about all night in the cold. Nobody ever gets down there anyway – so I went home to bed". Perhaps it as well for the peace of mind of nearby residents that the sidings have now all gone and that these emotive loads cannot now linger in station yards.

In 1972 the outlook for the branch actually improved with Essex County Council announcing plans for a new town at South Woodham Ferrers with an ultimate population of 15,000. It was estimated that by the early 1980s there would be 2,000 commuters per day from Woodham Ferrers. Essex County Council – together with three local councils – subsidised an experimentally restored Sunday service of nine trains each way for eight weeks from 12th August 1973: this was repeated between June and September 1974.

Permanent way problems continued to plague the Southminster branch and in February 1972 two coaches of a crowded four coach commuter train – the 7.23am from Southminster – left the rails just outside Fambridge station, causing damage to the track, although no-one was hurt. Buses were laid on to replace the train and a British Rail spokesman said that the cause of the derailment was unknown. The same thing had been said about the ballast train derailments at Althorne in 1967 and at Battlesbridge in 1968, and was to be said yet again in August 1974 when there was a spectacular crash at Althorne as the last four wagons and the brake van of a 22 wagon train carrying sand and gravel jumped the rails at 10.30pm, ripping up 180 yards of track. Fortunately there were no injuries, but once again, commuters were forced to make part of their journey by bus. There has since been an extensive relaying programme on the line. Relaying of the line continued, with sometimes four or five locomotives being used some weekends. December 1978 saw the section between Burnham on Crouch and Southminster concentrated on, with long welded rails replacing the old track.

By early 1974 the sand trains were reduced to working a conditional evening train on Mondays, Wednesdays and Fridays.

Spring 1976 saw more modernisation at the stations on the line when the old nameboards were removed and replaced with small 'continental type' boards. At Fambridge, there were nameboards from three eras. On the post was the new, small nameboard. On the grass beneath lay the large blue and white BR board, whilst beneath that was the black and white LNER board. An enquiry to Wickford station by a would-be purchaser of one of these eventually brought forth an answer from the National Railway Museum, York, that all obsolete nameboards from the line were to be transported to the museum and that anyone wishing to purchase should apply there. It seemed so ridiculous to him for the board to twice travel the length of the country only to finish up almost at its original location, that he took the matter no further.

In 1977 the Up branch bay platform at Wickford, normally used only in peak hours, was extended to accommodate five coach trains due to burgeoning passenger numbers: trains of this length were introduced from 9th January 1978.

In the autumn of 1977 Southminster and Fambridge stations (under pseudonyms) featured in BBC TV's 'Dick Emery Show'. This hilarious edition had as its theme the rivalry between the two stations in their efforts to win an award for the most efficient station on the line. At Fambridge various methods were used to disguise the down-at-heel condition of the premises, whilst Southminster was portrayed as the epitome of military style smartness, even the unfortunate commuters being ordered on to their train by numbers. Unfortunately, the efficiency of Southminster degenerated into a scene of chaos with fruit being thrown at railway staff and passengers and Fambridge won the award by sheer skulduggery. There had also been a serious cinema feature on Althorne station and its lady stationmaster in the early 1960s.

The real commuters were still not finding life on the line very happy however and in November 1978 almost one hundred of them invaded the supervisor's office

Battlesbridge station on 19th January 1974 after rationalisation: in later years even the brick shelter was to be demolished (Paddy Lacey)

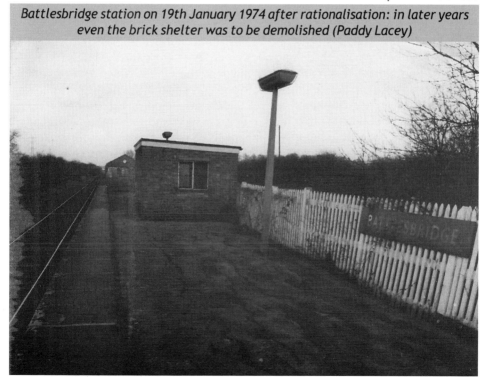

at Wickford station in an angry mood, their Southminster branch train having left without them. A petition demanding better service was made up for presentation to BR pointing out that despite assurances at Liverpool Street that their connection would await them at Wickford; it had gone when they arrived. Mr. Ray Spinks, the petition organiser, said "We have had enough, if you got something for your money it would be alright, but the service is terrible". A BR spokesman said that the trouble was caused by lack of communication between Wickford and Liverpool Street, which point may have already occurred to the frustrated commuters!

1979 started badly for the branch, with two Stratford based snowploughs being used to clear the branch on 1 January. The heating systems on the diesel multiple units left a lot to be desired, suffering from recurring failures. Cancellations, short formed trains and use of buses as substitutes happened regularly. It is believed that on one occasion around 350 passengers were crammed into a two car unit, which was substituting for what was normally a five car train. It is little surprise that the commuters were a far from happy group. Power failure on the main line caused an unusual working on 16 February though, when a diesel multiple unit formed a through service at 1703 from Liverpool Street to Southminster. Changes were made to the timetable in May 1979, with the old 0640 from Southminster being retimed to 0620, with an additional service leaving the terminus at 0702. This was aimed at improving the service, as well as easing the overcrowding that regularly occurred on the 0640 train. However, Sunday trains were reinstated permanently from May 1979 in a rare ray of hope.

The ballast traffic on the line ceased in early November 1978 – the pit at Southminster being exhausted – and once again fears arose for the line's future. In early 1979 a meeting was held at Latchingdon, the aim of which was to get the ballast from a new pit at Asheldham, only one and a half miles from Southminster, on to the railway and the heavy gravel lorries off Dengie's narrow and winding roads. Several village councils agreed to unite in fight and they were supported by Maldon's MP Mr John Wakeham, who arranged to meet British Rail for talks. For their part, BR had already agreed to make a detailed study of the matter and stated that they were interested in encouraging traffic to use the line.

It was also stated that the cost of getting the ballast trains moving again would be about £250,000 but the local councils were determined to eliminate the danger to life and limb arising from the daily forty or fifty lorry trips required to transport the same amount, particularly as in the harvest season considerable lorry traffic arises from the movement of some 1,500,000 tons of grain from the same area. It was suggested that the grain could also be carried by rail and that perhaps returning wagons could bring back animal feed. (Shades of the Thames barge!) As the line had in the past come near to closure due to lack of local support, it was felt that increased goods traffic could only be of benefit. Part of the battle was won when the ballast trains resumed in the spring of 1979, although only at a rate of one per day. However, this revival was not to last long, with the last loaded train being a special on 3 November 1979. A special train of empty wagons was worked away from Southminster on 6 November; the finality of the loss of traffic was sealed with the demolition of the overhead loading gantry on 13/14 December 1979.

The other Southminster line 'freight' – the trains of nuclear waste – came into the news again in June 1979 when allegations were made that a 50 ton container filled with nuclear waste was left unattended in Southminster station yard whilst children played nearby. A Health and Safety expert said that he thought that the safety precautions at the station were 'horrifying' and that the container had been left unguarded for forty-five minutes whilst children played in the siding behind it. He had begun his study of the nuclear waste transportation after receiving enquiries from an anxious railway worker and, after concluding his investigations, said that with the 'casual' security arrangements in force, sabotage or terrorism were very real risks.

In reply, the Central Electricity Generating Board (CEGB) denied that there was any risk from the container and said that there were three men in charge of the loading operation in the station yard, two of them being at the station enquiring about a train when the container was apparently unattended. The location of the third man was not disclosed.

The transport of flasks by rail was undoubtedly an emotional subject with local residents and no doubt questions and fears about them would continue to arise in the future, indeed the subject was reported upon in BBC TV's news bulletins on 23rd January 1980. Only three days later a protest march was held through the streets of London, the marchers voicing opposition to the rail transport of the containers through the capital. (Similar occurrences have yet to take place in the Dengie Hundred where the generating station provides employment for a large number of people from the surrounding area).

Film released by the CEGB showed the flasks being dropped from great heights and subject to intensive conflagration, apparently without damage, the Board insisting that the containers were virtually indestructible and that even if there was some seepage, the area affected would be minute. BR's Chief Operations Manager, Mr William Bradshaw said that their scientists were satisfied that the containers could withstand impacts of up to 30mph and temperatures up to 800 degrees Centigrade, and that research was being carried out by the CEGB with a view to doubling the impact safety factor. On the subject of terrorist attack, he admitted that it would be impossible to guard all the railway tracks which carried nuclear waste, but it was felt that the flasks would be proof against the impact of a bazooka type weapon. Proposals to install on the nuclear waste trains a radio communications system which could be used in the event of an accident or attack had been held up for at least a year by a dispute between guards and drivers as to who should operate the equipment.

Meanwhile, the inhabitants of the Dengie Hundred learned to live with the movement of the nuclear waste trains, running at irregular times and rarely seen by the casual observer and as over 4500 journeys have been made without incident since 1962, it was strange that in 1980 people should suddenly become concerned with the question of safety. The generating station was closed from February 1980 to 1981 due to cracks in the welded cooling ducts, and during this time the transport of nuclear waste dwindled. However, one of these trains was seen waiting in the passing loop at Fambridge in the summer of 1980.

The ageing diesel multiple units that were used on the branch continued to cause concern, particularly over reliability. On weekdays, four units were required for service: three three-car units and one two-car unit. Saturdays required just one three-car unit, whilst on winter Sundays there was no service. Faced with the rocketing price of fuel oil in the early eighties, together with increasing commuter traffic, electrification was desperately needed.

Following the experimental reintroduction of summer Sunday services in 1980, this was repeated again in 1981, with Maldon Council paying a subsidy of £667 to British Rail to help offset the losses that would otherwise have been incurred.

In September 1982 it was announced that a new concrete footbridge was to be built over the line between Eastern Road and Glendale Road in Burnham on Crouch to replace the old crumbling one. Work was carried out fairly quickly, and on 27 February 1983 the old bridge was demolished. The new bridge was of higher proportions than the old one, and gave sufficient clearance for overhead electric wires. Later on that year, on 13 November 1983, a signalman's error nearly gave the line its second electric train, when a train was wrongly signalled at Wickford: not surprisingly, it did not get far, soon running out of overhead wires!

Althorne station in the DMU era, before being destaffed (Paddy Lacey)

Chapter 5: Electrification and subsequent events

It was in 1984 that the long awaited news came that the line was to be electrified. Work was to start in late 1984, with completion targeted for May 1986. The total cost of the project was estimated at just under £3 million. After initial preparatory work, it was during the early hours of 26th November 1984 that work started on preparing the foundations for the overhead masts. The foundations were of steel tubes, driven into the ground by compressed air rams. These tubes were about two feet in diameter, and varied between five and nine feet in length according to the location. After the tubes were in place, four lugs were welded to the top of the tubes, and the overhead masts then attached. The first four masts were erected at Wickford. Contractors for the electrification work were Balfour Beatty (Power Construction) who also supplied the wires for installation by BR engineers.

Work continued at a satisfactory pace, and the piling work was completed on 7th March 1985, when the final three were placed at Woodham Ferrers. Five road bridges and two footbridges were raised or rebuilt at this time, to give sufficient clearance for the overhead wires. Platforms were extended at all locations, with some also being raised. Signalling alterations also took place, involving the closure of the line's signalboxes, and the removal of the fixed distant signals which were replaced by reflectorised distant boards. Automatic level crossings were installed at Althorne and South Woodham Ferrers. Access to the remains of the goods yard at Southminster for the nuclear flask traffic was moved, to be controlled from a new two lever ground frame operated with an Annett's key. Considerable locomotive activity took place on the branch as part of this construction work, with a Class 08 diesel shunter being outbased at Southminster. This was used to power the electrification train, which usually consisted of four coaches and one cable wagon. Regular changeovers of the shunter had to take place, usually because the windows had become a target for local vandals.

The first wires were installed on 14th April 1985 when approximately four miles of earth return wire was erected between Althorne and Southminster. On the same day, the new concrete footbridge was installed at Fambridge. Contact wire was installed first near Althorne on 23rd June 1985, thus commencing the final stages of electrification work. Level crossings were converted to automatic operation as part of a gradual process, although not before new crossing gates had to be installed at Woodham Ferrers on 30th June 1985 after a DMU collided with them – a not unknown occurrence.

From 8th September 1985, the overhead wiring train was stabled at Wickford, due to work being carried out at Southminster. Initially, run round facilities were withdrawn there: new facilities were provided in the goods yard, rather than in the station itself. Whilst this work was ongoing, the opportunity was taken to overhaul the overhead gantry used for loading the nuclear flasks. Within a month, these works were complete. By the end of the year, the only work still outstanding was bridgework at Burnham on Crouch and near Southminster, together with the final connection to the rest of the overhead system at Wickford – plus the associated signalling work. At 0001 on 17th March 1986 current was switched on to the overhead wires between Wickford and Southminster with the full electric service scheduled for introduction two months later. Sunday 23rd March saw the first test runs of an electric train, albeit not in passenger service. From 14th April 1986 the 0629 Wickford to Southminster and 0714 Southminster to Shenfield were booked to be worked by an electric unit: 24th April saw test runs being carried out on the branch, using electric unit 307108. But all was not quite smooth running: services on the line were disrupted for three days in April in a dispute over the running of the new electric services. The big day finally came on 12th May 1986 when the full electric service was introduced. The service continued to run as a shuttle in the off peak between Wickford and Southminster, with through trains in the peak hours.

1989 saw the centenary of the branch, with two special events being operated. On 1st July, a special party of Maldon Council representatives, councillors, officers, British Rail officials, and Dennis Swindale (author of this book) boarded the 0956 departure from Wickford. The front coach was commandeered for use as a mobile hospitality unit, and at each stop on the line representatives from the parish councils that the line passes through (Rettendon, South Woodham Ferrers, Purleigh, Stow Maries, North Fambridge, Latchingdon, Althorne and Burnham) boarded. Arrival at Southminster was a significant affair: to the sounds of horns hooting, the platform was full of a large crowd of school children, together with the Southminster parish council. At the controls of the train on the final approach was a ten year old Southminster schoolboy, who had won the opportunity to drive the train in a painting competition. A tent in the station forecourt was dispensing free refreshments. A preserved London bus then took the assembled dignitaries to the local sports ground, where various speeches were made before they were taken on to Mangapps Farm Railway Museum at Burnham for a visit. At Mangapps Farm is the frame from Southminster signal box, which is now connected to some of the signals recovered from the branch. At the conclusion of the visit, the vintage bus returned the party to Burnham Station. Keith Munnion, Chairman of Maldon District Council summed up the proceedings, saying "the day has been very successful indeed with British Rail and Maldon District Council combining to mark this special celebration of a branch line that has meant so much to the people of the Crouch Valley for one hundred years".

The second part of the centenary celebrations took place on 28th August 1989, the August Bank Holiday. As part of the event – which also commemorated the centenary of the line from Shenfield to Southend Victoria, a special ticket was available priced at £3 (£1.50 for children) which gave unlimited travel between Shenfield, Southend Victoria and Southminster. The big event of the day was the steaming of the preserved Class N7 locomotive No.69621 (based at the East Anglian Railway Museum at Chappel & Wakes Colne, near Colchester) at Southend, where there was also a large exhibition of rolling stock and other items. But the Southminster line was not forgotten: services for the day were operated by the preserved Class 306 electric multiple unit, dating back to 1949. In addition, there was a free vintage bus from Burnham station to Mangapps Farm Railway Museum.

In 1994 the Woodham Chronicle newspaper reported that local teenagers had started a campaign to convert the disused station house at Woodham Ferrers into a youth centre, albeit – as it turned out – unsuccessfully.

1997 saw relaying take place of around five miles of track at the eastern end of the branch between Fambridge and Burnham on Crouch, which included the construction of a new siding for Grant Rail, the infrastructure contractor. This removed the last section of jointed track on the branch. Part of the empty station house at Southminster was used as an office for the duration of this work, during which the last two trains of each evening were replaced by buses. The same year saw the nuclear flask workings change from Class 31 to Class 37 haulage: the last Class 31 working is believed to have been on 16th January 1997 when 31439 *North Yorkshire Moors Railway* worked the service.

From 1st January 1997 as part of the railway privatisation process the line became operated by First Bus under the name First Great Eastern. On 29th June 1997 Hertfordshire Railtours operated the 'Arch Weaver' mystery tour as 1Z72 0930 Liverpool Street to Waterloo utilising a Great Western Trains liveried HST set with power cars 43185 *Great Western* and 43012: this tour traversed both the Southminster and Southend Victoria branches.

Southminster station at possibly its busiest time ever on 29th June 1997 when an InterCity High Speed Train visited the branch (Roland Shaw)

1998 saw the burning down of the station house at Wickford on November 4th, in what is believed to have been an arson attack: the remains were subsequently demolished. From October 1998 Direct Rail Services (DRS) took over operation of the nuclear flask trains, using pairs of Class 20 locomotives. However, on 1st December 1999 British Nuclear Fuels Ltd announced that the Magnox nuclear power station at Bradwell would close in March 2002, with decommissioning taking up to three years to complete thereafter. The same year First Bus changed to First Group to reflect their expansion into rail activities.

The branch has gained a reputation for vandalism and disorder in recent years: CCTV cameras were installed at Southminster, Burnham on Crouch and Woodham Ferrers in 2000. This was followed in early 2002 by the introduction of piped music at a number of First Great Eastern stations, including Burnham on Crouch, between 1600 and 2300 each evening in an attempt to deter youths hanging around station property and causing damage.

On 6th May 2002 the branch saw the return for one day of steam. Leaving Liverpool Street at 1054 was a train top and tailed with Class 4 76079 and LMS Class 5 45407. After visiting Southend Victoria from 1158 to 1335 it ran to Wickford before continuing to Southminster, where it arrived at 1445. Departing again at 1525, it returned to Southend Victoria before the last leg back to London. At the

45407 near Fambridge on 6th May 2002 (G. D. King)

same time, First Great Eastern's vintage Class 306 unit was working on the branch, forming the 1332 Wickford to Southminster and 1412 return.

The 1816 Liverpool Street to Southminster train collided with a farm tractor on an open crossing at Hogwells Chase, near Woodham Ferrers, on 12th September 2002. The eight car train, formed of 321445+321335, was travelling at around 45mph and sustained serious damage. The tractor was destroyed, but the driver managed to jump clear. The train driver, the tractor driver and one passenger were taken to hospital with minor injuries. The train remained on the tracks but the impact brought down the overhead power equipment, and passengers had to be detrained at the accident scene and taken home by road. All branch trains were replaced by buses until 0830 the following morning to allow repairs to the overhead equipment. Subsequently, two farm labourers appeared at Chelmsford Crown Court on 6th May 2003 charged with causing the collision: they were found guilty and sentenced to do 100 hours community service each.

From July 2003 there were some additional nuclear flask trains to Southminster which ran in the early morning before the first passenger train. The regular Thursday train also ran to Southminster before the first trains, but returned in the booked path.

Due to engineering work, the train service was suspended from Monday 19th to Wednesday 21st January 2004 and again from Monday 26th to Wednesday 28th January 2004 from 0930 to 1530 each day. From 1st April 2004 under the re-franchising First Group lost the franchise to National Express, who originally marketed their East Anglian operations under the name 'One', but in 2008 re-branded themselves as 'National Express East Anglia'.

The final recorded nuclear flask train working took place on Thursday 31st August 2006, when the locomotives used were 20306 and 20309.

On 20th May 2007 two stations changed their names slightly to reflect their true location, with Fambridge becoming North Fambridge and Woodham Ferrers becoming South Woodham Ferrers. For the former there was an official ceremony held on 12th July 2007 in a joint venture between 'one' Railway and North Fambridge Parish Council.

Burnham on Crouch station made the news in Autumn 2007 twice – and for rather different reasons. On 10th October 2007 a tea party was held at the station as a celebration of the achievement of station adopters in Essex, who are local people who help with the upkeep of floral displays and report faults and other defects to 'one' Railway. Burnham was selected as the location as it had recently won the Anglia in Bloom best station award.

Also new technology came to Burnham when it became one of the first stations to have a 'Mosquito' device installed. This device generates a pulsed near ultrasonic tone at around 16khz, which is close to the limit of the hearing range of young people under about 25. Whilst it is not painful, it does become irritating after about five to ten minutes with the result that young people move away rather than loiter at the station.

It was felt in the late seventies that the future survival of the line would depend to a great extent upon the nuclear power station at Bradwell. With the closure of Bradwell power station freight traffic is no more, but the electrification and increasing passenger numbers would appear to ensure that the line has an assured future, with all stations – except Battlesbridge – seeing growth in passenger numbers. In early 2008 – as this edition was being finalised – there were press reports of a possible new nuclear power station at Bradwell: should this come to fruition then it is likely that some construction material will be moved by rail as well as, in due course, the return of the nuclear waste traffic.

The memories of the line will always remain, whatever happens in the future. Now under its fifth ownership with the privatisation of the railways completed, it is operated by 'one' – part of the National Express empire. Those who use and have used the line think of it as a friendly one. To many the memories remain of waiting rooms with polished floors, shiny furniture, vases of fresh flowers, and roaring fires in winter. Now station staff have been reduced, with only Burnham and South Woodham Ferrers retaining a booking office on Monday to Friday mornings. Shelter for the waiting passengers has been reduced at most stations to a primitive nature, but the line still lives and it is to be hoped that it will continue to serve the community well into its second century.

Chapter 6: Locomotives and Rolling Stock

The Southminster line has been host to a wide variety of motive power, in steam days ranging from small tender and tank locomotives to heavy express engines.

In the early period most of the branch passenger trains were hauled by GER Class 61 0-4-4T and Class M15 2-4-2T (LNER Class F4) locomotives. Designed by William Adams, fifty Class 61 locomotives were built between 1875-8, so were at least eleven years old when they came to the Southminster and Maldon West lines. They were built variously by Neilson, Kitson and R. Stephenson and at first had backless cabs, which must have been hard on their crews when the locomotives were running in reverse in bad weather. A rear weatherboard was later fitted which separated the cab from the small bunker and by the time that they came into service on the Southminster branch their original livery of black with red lining had been replaced with the passenger locomotive blue. They carried two tons of coal and 1000 gallons of water and weighed nearly 49 tons. Withdrawals began in 1906 and the last was scrapped in 1913, so none survived for the Grouping.

The Class F4 2-4-2T locomotives (later rebuilt as F5s) were not popular, as they were fitted with 'Joys' valve gear, which did not suit them and caused heavy and rapid coal consumption, hence their nickname of 'Gobblers'. They also gave a very rough ride, which did not endear them to their crews. They weighed over 53 tons and carried $3\frac{1}{2}$ tons of coal and 1200 gallons of water. Despite their unpopularity, 118 engines in original condition were taken into the

Y14 647 working the 3.5pm ECS ex Southminster near Wickford on 22nd April 1911 (Ken Nunn Collection, courtesy Locomotive Club of Great Britain)

LNER at the 1923 Grouping and 37 remained in service in 1945, some remaining in service until replaced by diesel units. Class T19 2-4-0 and T19 rebuilt 4-4-0s were visitors to the branch in the early years of the twentieth century.

The best known tank locomotives to work the Southminster line were the Class L77 (LNER Class N7) 0-6-2Ts. These were very efficient engines, designed by A.J. Hill and first produced in 1915 for the London suburban traffic. They weighed 61 tons 12 cwt and carried 3½ tons of coal and 1600 gallons of water. The first twenty-two of the class were built at Stratford Works, the last ten being finished after the 1923 Grouping, and the another 112 were built by the LNER at other works. They were highly thought of by the LNER and, slightly modified, became the standard loco for the Great Eastern section London suburban services. The twenty two Stratford built engines were withdrawn between 1958 and 1961 and were the last type of steam passenger locomotives to work the Southminster line. One of the engaging features of the ex-GER engines was the Westinghouse brake pump which at the end of a journey panted in a manner reminiscent of a runner who had just completed a race. Luckily, this evocative sound will once more delight our ears as N7/4 0-6-2T locomotive No. 69621 was restored to full working order at the East Anglian Railway Museum at Chappel and Wakes Colne Station, Colchester, Essex,: at present it is on long term loan to the North Norfolk Railway at Sheringham.

Another type of locomotive frequently to be seen working either goods or passenger trains on the line was the GER Class Y14 0-6-0 (LNER Class J15). These small tender locomotives were to be found all over the GER system and the class had a lifespan of eighty years, being introduced in 1883 and the last withdrawn in 1963. Designed by T.W. Wordsell, they weighed over 67 tons and their tenders held 5 tons of coal and 2640 gallons of water. They were popular with their footplate crews and could handle with relative ease quite heavy freight trains, whilst light branch passenger trains were an easy task. The J15s looked the epitome of a country branch line locomotive with their long chimneys and low boilers, and to recall the eastern counties rural railway scene in the mind's eye is more often than not to visualise a J15, white smoke trailing from the tall chimney, leisurely chuffing its way through the country greenery at the head of a train of varnished coaches. Happily, J15 No. 564 has been preserved and renovated and can be seen at the North Norfolk Railway headquarters at Sheringham, Norfolk.

These were the most usual steam locomotives to be seen upon the Southminster branch, but many other types visited the line, including a single Tilbury 4-4-2T No. 41952, in the mid-1950s. It was sent there from Southend shed, but was a poor performer. Class J17 and Class J20 0-6-0 locomotives were occasional visitors and sometimes appeared on freight trains. The J17 was designed by J. Holden, ninety were built and the last was withdrawn in 1963. They have been described as 'very lively and high spirited'. The J20, designed by A.J. Hill, was for some time the largest and most powerful class of 0-6-0 locomotive in the country and some considered them to be one of Mr Hill's best designs. so sometimes to be seen were the Class T26 (LNER Class E4) 2-4-0 'Intermediates', another Holden design and used for secondary passenger, cross country and general branch work. These splendid little locomotives were easy runners with good acceleration, the last being withdrawn in 1960. This was No. 62785 (GER No. 490) and it was by then the sole 2-4-0 engine to remain in service in England. Now it is restored to its former glory and can be seen in the National Railway Museum at York.

The largest locomotives used upon the branch – usually on the through trains from Liverpool Street – were the 'Claud Hamilton' Class 4-4-0 and the '1500' Class 4-6-0 express passenger engines, LNER Classes D14, 15 and 16 and B12. These magnificent locomotives were designed by J. Holden and S.D. Holden respectively and represented the ultimate in GER design. They were rebuilt by the LNER and nearly all survived to be taken into British Rail stock. The first 'Claud' was so named in honour of Lord Claud Hamilton, the then Chairman of the Great Eastern Railway, and was built at Stratford. For eleven years the class was the mainstay of the GER heavy main line passenger services and it was not until 1920 that there were enough 4-6-0 locomotives to ease the strain on the 'Clauds'. Many of the original 'Clauds', (later to be LNER Class D14) were adapted to burn liquid fuel, carrying 715 gallons of waste oil, but only 11 tons of coal. The oil used was waste from the production of the oil gas used for carriage lighting and was difficult to dispose of by other means. Some were given a larger boiler, a Belpaire firebox and other improvements, including superheating and became LNER Class D15, then in 1922 the further improved 'Super Clauds' (LNER Class D16) appeared. After the 1923 Grouping the LNER rebuilt many of the 'Clauds' to their standards and they became known as Class D16/3, the beautiful GER blue paint giving way to LNER green and the standard LNER chimney replacing the original. It is a compliment to the class that Sir Nigel Gresley decided to retain and modernise them and that they remained in service long after nationalisation, by which time they were finished in fully lined-out black livery. The last was withdrawn in 1960.

It is a great pity that none was selected for preservation and restoration to its GER splendour, but one can imagine the magnificent picture of a 'Claud' heading its train across the Crouch marshland in the summer sunlight – a vision of deep GER blue, brilliant red coupling rods and frames, a profusion of glinting brass and of the colourful GER coat of arms mounted proudly on the front splasher. Such a sight will not be seen on the Southminster line again.

If the 'Clauds' were the apex of design by J. Holden, the '1500' Class (LNER Class B12) 4-6-0 locomotives were that of S.D. Holden. They were a development of the later 'Clauds', being similar in appearance but with smaller driving wheels and larger smoke boxes. The first forty one of the class were built at Stratford between 1911 and 1917, the final total being built amounting to eighty one engines. When in LNER ownership, the B12s came into three groups, B12/1 and B12/2 for the locomotives as originally built, and the B12/3 for the Gresley rebuilds. They were a splendid sight in their LNER green livery and lasted well into BR days, the last being withdrawn in 1960 and subsequently purchased by the Midland and Great Northern Joint Railway Society. It is a happy thought that this magnificent locomotive has been restored and taken into use on the North Norfolk Railway.

61569 at Woodham Ferrers on 16th September 1956
(J. Frankland, EARM Collection)

Apart from the Tilbury Tank, the only other non-GER steam locomotives to visit the Southminster branch were the LNER B17 'Sandringham' Class 4-6-0 express passenger locomotives, designed by Sir Nigel Gresley and introduced in 1928. The story persists – and it has come from several sources – that a 'Britannia' Class 4-6-2 locomotive once hauled a passenger train as far as Southminster, some say at the time of the opening of Bradwell Nuclear Power Station, and there seems to be no reason that this should not have been so as the 'Britannias' had a route availability of 8. This would certainly have been the heaviest and largest type of steam locomotive to traverse the branch.

The earliest type of passenger coaches used on the branch were four and six wheelers – GER secondary stock, teak finished and Westinghouse braked, the for wheelers remaining in use on branch lines until 1905 and the six wheelers much longer. The early coaches were equipped with gas lighting, but by the early 1900s this had been replaced by the more economical incandescent lights. No less than four examples of GER nineteenth century wooden passenger stock are preserved at Chappel and Wakes Colne Station including a four-wheel first class coach of 1878 and a six-wheel full passenger brake van.

By the 1930s, bogie coaches, still of teak construction, had been introduced to the line and three of these would form a normal branch train, usually a non-corridor brake/third class, a first/third class semi-corridor and a full third class. The weekend London trains, which divided at Wickford, consisted of nine corridor coaches.

ACV lightweight railcar at Southminster in September 1953
(Frank Church collection, courtesy Essex Bus Enthusiasts Group)

The experimental ACV four wheeled railcar was used on the branch on Mondays to Fridays from 21st September 1953 to 9th October 1953. Diesel multiple units replaced steam passenger trains from 11th June 1956 and timings were improved. The usual diesel multiple unit trains had two or three coaches; classes noted on the branch included Derby Lightweight, Metro-Cammell Class 101 and Cravens Class 105 units. At certain busy times, five coach trains were to be seen, which posed problems at stations such as Althorne and Battlesbridge, which had shortened platforms. At Althorne, for instance, platform space only existed for three carriages and the leading two came to a stand over the level crossing.

Freight trains on the branch were normally worked by either Class 37 or Class 47 diesel locomotives, although there was a rare visitor on 29th November 1978 when Class 50 No. 50005 'Collingwood' visited the branch. On 26th February 1983 a railtour from Plymouth visited Southminster, hauled by Class 50 50030.

The electric service began with a mixture of Class 302 and 307 units. Class 312s only operated when the 0715 from Southminster began operating as a twelve coach train in May 1987. In 1992, this was reduced to eight coaches and Class 312s no longer saw regular use on the branch. However, from 1st June 1996 Class 312s made a reappearance on the branch, when the 0715 from Southminster was once again restored to a twelve coach formation. The purpose of operating twelve coaches is to increase capacity for customers joining at Woodham Ferrers – where many were unable to get a seat when the train was formed of only eight

The modern scene on the Southminster line: 321332 and 321307 at Fambridge in July 2005

coaches. The train could not be formed of Class 321s because the Department of Transport will not allow 'sliding door' stock to call at stations where the platform length is shorter than the train: no such restriction applies to slam door stock. This was subsequently resolved by the fitting of selective door operation to some Class 321 units.

The first Class 321s were introduced in December 1988, and were progressively slotted into train diagrams from that time onwards until May 1989 when the entire fleet was operational. A couple of peak period Southend line diagrams continued to be operated by Class 307s until their final withdrawal from the area in January 1990.

Nuclear flask trains tended to operate latterly with two Class 20 locomotives, but from time to time a Class 20 operated with a Class 37. One such occasion, for example, was on 22nd April 2004 when 20310 worked the train with 37059. On 5th May 2005, 20306, 20312 and 37059 were on the flask train; on 17th November 2005 came the unprecedented and, as far as is known, only time when three Class 37 locomotives were used, with 37059+37069+37609.

The final recorded use of twelve car Class 312 formation was on 28th June 2004: on 1st July 2004 came the first recorded use of twelve car Class 321 units on the 0715 from Southminster, with 321441+321443+321448 in use.

Chapter 7: Signalling

Together with the other New Essex Lines, the Southminster branch was equipped with the block telegraph from opening and there was a signal box at each station. The train staff and ticket system was in use, all the intermediate stations – with the exception of Battlesbridge and Althorne – being staff stations. Each station was equipped with home, distant and starter signals of the lower quadrant type, whilst the passing loops were fitted with low disc-type shunt signals, which survived well into the 1950s. Most of the post signals had by then long been replaced by the upper quadrant type, the last original GER specimen lingering until the early 1960s, at Althorne. When the Southend line was electrified in 1958, colour light signals replaced the old semaphores, those at Wickford being fitted with indicators showing 'B' for branch and 'M' for main line. The bank down to Wickford station and the junction is protected by a distant and two home signals as a precaution against over-running.

In the latter days of diesel operation, the only signal boxes remaining on the branch were at Southminster and Fambridge, the latter being the point at which the line is divided into two sections: the Fambridge to Wickford section being worked with Tyer's key equipment and the Fambridge to Southminster section by Railway Signal Company's brass staff. All distant signals were fixed.

As part of the electrification work, all signalling was modernised. Control of the line was passed to Wickford signal box, with all signals becoming of the modern colour light variety. The former fixed distant signals were replaced by reflectorised distant boards. Fambridge and Southminster signalboxes were closed on 19th January 1986, with the demolition men moving in during February 1986: the frame from Southminster has been preserved at Mangapps Railway Museum. Subsequently, with further stages of the Great Eastern resignalling project, control has passed to Liverpool Street IECC – Wickford signalbox closing on 22nd August 1983 and being demolished in 1992.

From late on 23rd October 1992 until early on 26th October 1992 the branch service was replaced by buses whilst the trailing crossover at the London end of Wickford station was removed and the ground frame taken out of use. A new facing crossover was installed, clipped out of use pending commissioning.

From 27th to 30th November 1992 train services were again replaced by buses whilst new signalling, controlled from Liverpool Street signal box, was brought into use on the branch and as far as the London side of Wickford station. At this time Wickford signal box was retained to supervise down line signals between Mountnessing Junction and Wickford. The new facing crossover installed the previous month was commissioned.

Chapter 8: Train services

The halcyon GER days for the line were in 1914 with the publication of the 'Radical Alterations' timetable. This showed ten return workings on the branch weekdays, with the 8.23am arriving at Liverpool Street at 9.46am, having stopped at Burnham on Crouch, Woodham Ferrers, Wickford, Billericay, Shenfield and Brentwood.

In the summer 1922 timetable there were nine down trains Mondays to Fridays and ten on Saturdays. There were eight up trains Mondays to Fridays and nine on Saturdays. Sunday services consisted of three trains each way. The fastest journey time in the up direction was 99 minutes on the 8.8 am train from Southminster: in the down direction it was 81 minutes by the 4.15 train Mondays to Fridays.

Pre Second World War there were nine trains each way weekdays, the only through service from Southminster to Liverpool Street was the 8.18am arriving at 9.50am. On Saturdays only there was a through train from Liverpool Street at 1.27pm calling at Billericay, Wickford and Burnham on Crouch, arriving at Southminster at 2.43pm.

In December 1949 there were 10 down and 12 up trains Monday to Friday, with the fastest service being the 12.05pm Southminster to Liverpool Street, changing at Shenfield, which took 90 minutes. The only weekday through train was the 5.48am from Southminster, which arrived at Liverpool Street at 7.28am.

The Winter 1962-3 timetable saw sixteen trains each way Mondays to Fridays: all trains called at all stations apart from one up evening train which called only at Burnham and Fambridge. Saturdays saw fourteen trains each way whilst on Sundays there were eight down and seven up trains. The first down train on Sundays started from Stratford, all other trains only working on the branch. The fastest journey times Mondays to Fridays were 70 minutes up (by the 0852 ex Southminster): in the down direction, it was the same (leaving London at 1018 or 1218).

The 1967-8 timetable saw fourteen down and fifteen up trains Mondays to Fridays. All down trains called at all stations, but two evening up trains omitted Battlesbridge and a further evening up train called only at Burnham and Fambridge. Saturdays saw thirteen trains each way whilst Sundays enjoyed ten trains each way – although two each way did not run between Southminster and Burnham. All trains operated purely on the branch, with the exception of the first down train on Sundays which started from Stratford. The fastest journey times possible to and from London were 70 minutes in the up direction (by the 0852 ex Southminster Mondays to Fridays); in the down direction 68 minutes (leaving London at 1754).

From 14 May 1990, a further improvement was made to the train service on the branch when off-peak services started running through to and from Liverpool Street, instead of just in the peak hours

In 1999 there were 22 trains each way Monday to Friday, with the fastest journey time between Southminster and Liverpool Street covering the 45 miles 42 chains in 63 minutes. In 2001 the Metro service was extended through to Southminster hourly off peak.

From December 2005 the off peak timetable was again revised so that the branch was no longer served by an hourly extension of the Metro service. In its place came an hourly Class 321 Southminster to Shenfield (Wickford on Sundays) service: whilst requiring a change of trains it does offer a faster service with better trains which include toilet facilities. This is still the service pattern today.

For many years one round trip did not operate on the branch on Thursday lunchtimes to accommodate the flask train: with the closure of Bradwell power station this gap was filled from December 2007.

> Passengers for Burnham—on—Crouch, Althorne and Fambridge must travel in the front eight coaches.
>
> For Battlesbridge passengers must travel in front four coaches

Advice of short platforms and where to sit in the train: sign at Southminster seen in July 2005

SOUTHMINSTER BRANCH
GOODS FACILITIES AT 1923 GROUPING
"S" = Southern Division   Closing Times for Goods at Stations - 5 p.m. (Sats. 12.30 p.m.)

STATION	DIVISION	L LIVE STOCK	W WATER SUPPLY FOR ANIMALS IN TRANSIT	D LOADING DOCK	F FURNITURE VANS ETC. ON WHEELS	R ROUND TIMBERS	V LIFT VANS ETC. REQUIRING CRANE POWER	CRANES TONS	DUCKHAM TONS	WEIGH BRIDGES T TRUCK / C CART	WEIGH BRIDGES TONS	WEIGHING MACHINES TONS	WEIGHING MACHINES CWTS	S GOODS SHED / G SEPARATE GRANARIES (NO. OF QRS OF GRAIN EACH STATION CAN STORE)	LK LOCK UP FOR SMALL PACKAGES / T TURNTABLE	WHO PERFORMS CARTAGE (A AGENT / C COMPANY)
Wickford	S	L	W	D	F	R	V	-	-	- C	7	1	0	---	LK -	A
Battlesbridge	S	L	W	D	F	-	V	1½	-	T -	20	1	0	S 400	LK -	-
Woodham Ferrers	S	L	W	D	F	R	V	-	-	T -	20	1	0	- -	LK -	-
Hogwell Siding	S	L	-	-	-	-	-	-	-	- -	-	-	-	- -	- -	-
Fambridge	S	L	W	D	F	-	V	-	-	- -	-	1	0	- -	LK -	-
Althorne	S	L	-	D	F	-	V	-	-	T -	20	1	0	- -	LK -	-
Creeksea Ferry Siding	S	-	-	-	-	-	-	-	-	- -	-	-	-	- -	- -	-
Burnham-on-Crouch	S	L	W	D	F	-	V	1½	-	T -	20	1	0	S 500	LK -	A
Southminster	S	L	W	D	F	R	V	1½	-	- -	20	1	0	S 500	LK T	A

Appendix 1

Details of work carried out by Mr Middleton Senior

(Copied from the Carlisle Journal, 27th February 1891)

    We regret to announce the death of Mr. Thomas Middleton at his residence, Warner's, Burnham, Essex, on the 2nd inst., the result of a railway accident on Wednesday last. The deceased gentleman was on the line near Wickford and had stepped out of the way of a goods train which was approaching, but did not observe that an empty carriage train was moving towards him on the adjoining line; he was knocked down and several of the carriages passed over his right leg which was so much injured that it had to be amputated above the knee. The shock to his system was too great and he gradually sank after the operation.

    Mr. Middleton, who was born at Warmfield, near Wakefield, has been closely connected with the construction of many of the most important public works in the country.

    About the year 1841 he had charge of the Midland Railway from Oakenshaw to Marbro' and afterwards of the construction of part of the Leeds and Thirsk and the Stour Valley lines. Subsequently he was appointed on behalf of the contractors to the supervision of the building of Birkenhead Docks in 1850, and of the Swansea

Dock in 1854. In 1857 Mr. Middleton entered the service of the late Mr. Thomas Nelson, contractor of this city and during his connection with that gentleman was entrusted with the construction of the first dock at Silloth and (in conjunction with Mr. C. Moses), the Portpatrick Railway and new piers and branch lines at Stranraer; the Holme Head Bay and Bolton branches for the Maryport and Carlisle Railway.

On completion of these works he removed to Sussex where he had charge of the construction of 22 miles of new line for the London, Brighton and South Coast Railway; but owing to the crisis of 1866 the Railway Company were obliged to suspend the works owing to the difficulty of raising capital and subsequently to abandoning the undertaking altogether.

About the year 1868, Mr. Middleton returned to the north having become connected with Mr. Walter Scott, contractor, of Newcastle on Tyne, and the relations then begun have continued until his death, a period of 23 years. During this time he superintended the construction of many works in the North Eastern District, including new railways in Cleveland, the extensive new deep water docks and entrances at West Hartlepool and branch railways and widenings, including the new railway bridge over the River Tees at Stockton. With reference to his connection with Silloth 30 years ago it is interesting to note that the construction of the second dock at Silloth was carried out on behalf of the firm by his son, Mr. J.T. Middleton, on whose removal to the South of England, Mr. Middleton took charge and completed the works and the new railway bridge over the river Waver at Abbey Junction.

Messrs. Walter Scott and Co., having obtained a contract to construct 40 miles of railway in Essex for the Great Eastern Railway Co., Mr. Middleton was placed in charge of the Burnham section, and on completion, took charge of the maintenance of the whole lines, and it was while in the execution of his duty in this position that he met with the fatal accident described.

Mr. Middleton had many warm friends in Carlisle and the neighbourhood, who deeply sympathise with his widow and family.

Just two examples of relics from the Southminster line that are on display at Mangapps Railway Museum at Burnham on Crouch, which is well worth a visit. For more information on the Museum, telephone 01621 784898 or visit their website at http://www.mangapps.co.uk